Violence: Prevention and Treatment in Groups

The *Social Work with Groups* series

Series Editors: Catherine P. Papell and Beulah Rothman

Violence: Prevention and Treatment in Groups

George S. Getzel
Editor

The Haworth Press
New York • London

Violence: Prevention and Treatment in Groups has also been published as *Social Work with Groups*, Volume 11, Number 3 1988.

The Haworth Press, Inc., 12 West 32 Street, New York, NY 10001
EUROSPAN/Haworth, 3 Henrietta Street, London WC2E 8LU England

Library of Congress Cataloging-in-Publication Data

Violence : prevention and treatment in groups / George S. Getzel, editor.
    p. cm.
    "Has also been published as Social work with groups, volume 11, number 3, 1988" – T.p. verso.
    Includes bibliographical references.
    ISBN 0-86656-848-4
    1. Social group work – United States. 2. Family social work – United States. 3. Group psychotherapy – United States. 4. Family psychotherapy – United States. 5. Violence – United States – Prevention. I. Getzel, George S.
HV45.V54   1988
362.8'8 – dc 19   88-19171
                                    CIP

Violence: Prevention and Treatment in Groups

CONTENTS

FROM THE WORLD OF PRACTICE

ABOUT THE EDITOR

George S. Getzel, DSW, is Professor at Hunter College School of Social Work in New York City. As a consultant and author, Dr. Getzel's interests include group work and social work with the elderly, as well as assistance to AIDS patients and families of homicide victims. A Fellow of the Gerontological Society of America, Dr. Getzel is a co-editor of *Gerontological Social Work Practice in the Community* (1985) and *Gerontological Social Work Practice in Long-Term Care* (1983), both Haworth publications. He is also Chair of the National Association of Social Work Task Force on AIDS in New York City.

EDITORIAL

George Getzel, in his frequent contributions in this field, has called attention to and clarified a number of unexplored areas of human concern for social work with groups. For example, co-authored with Diego Lopez was the first paper in professional literature on groupwork practice with AIDS patients and their significant others.[1] The contribution of groupwork to this compelling contemporary problem was carefully documented by the authors' own direct practice. Their work has provided guideposts for practitioners and volunteers who are striving to offer meaningful services to those who are threatened by or suffering with AIDS.

Always unafraid to challenge disturbing problems, Getzel earlier had presented a practice paper on groupwork with parents of homicide victims.[2] In that paper Getzel and his co-author, Rosemary Masters, traced the group themes as the members struggled together with the profound trauma in surviving the violent death of a loved one. The insightful quality of the presentation of the practice and the power of the conceptualizations are rooted in the authors' closeness to the demanding nature of the work for the groupworker, as well as the pain of the experience for the member clients themselves. Getzel is ever mindful in all of his writings of the accessibility of his ideas to those who wish to use them.

For these reasons we have invited George Getzel to develop a special book related to groupwork practice with victims of violence. The depth and quality of this special book have more than met our expectations. We are sure that our readers will be grateful to Dr. Getzel, as we are, for his bringing together such timely informative accounts of practice and research.

CP
BR

NOTES

1. "Groupwork with Teams of Volunteers Serving People with AIDS." Vol. X, No.4, Winter 1987.
2. "Groupwork with Parents of Homicide Victims." Vol. VI, No. 2, Summer 1983.

Violence, Social Work, and Groups: An Overview

George S. Getzel

Fear of violent crime insinuates itself deeply into our everyday lives. Our conversations touch or dwell on the latest victim of personal violence – a woman battered by her husband in the house down the street, the elderly widow raped and beaten for her few dollars and the teenager shot by an angry man sensing he is about to be robbed. The routines of our daily lives are also influenced by the fear of becoming a victim of crime. We walk down a street only at certain hours or feel more comfortable living in a building which has an array of devices to prevent the illegal entry of a stranger. It is difficult to put these thoughts about victimization to rest, while we also know there are no fail-safe systems to counter each and every crime of personal harm.

THE EMERGENCE OF THE CRIME VICTIM

Although preoccupation with crime and the criminal has had a long history in the discipline of criminology and social work practice in the courts and correctional systems, a concern with violence and its victims has only surfaced in a significant way in the last fifteen years.

Recently, the mass media has been a powerful source of the public awareness of victimization through its portrayal in specific and graphic details of the frequency and the character of violent crimes

---

George S. Getzel, DSW, is Professor, Hunter College School of Social Work, 129 East 79th Street, New York, NY 10012.

such as spousal battering, child abuse and child molestation and abduction. Although in the wake of some horrific incident we may be prompted to discuss the prospect of victimization, the most common reaction to criminal violence to ourselves and others in the longer term is denial, which allows us to resume the routines of life with a minimum of emotional dislocation. Denial with its requisite beliefs and illusions buttresses us against threats to our ideology of personal well-being.

SOCIAL CONTEXT OF VICTIMIZATION

Thinking about criminal victimization must be seen within the broad social context of violence: war, genocide and political terrorism are witnessed, if not directly, vicariously on television every day by young and old alike. The "other-ness" of this exposure to violence may peak our awareness momentarily only to lull us into psychological numbness.

Political philosopher Hannah Arendt (1969, 8) in her classic essay *On Violence* wrote,

> No one engaged in thought about history and politics can remain unaware of the enormous role violence has always played in human affairs, and it is at first glance rather surprising that violence has been singled out so seldom for special consideration (in the last edition of the *Encyclopedia of Social Sciences* violence does not even rate an entry). This shows to what extent violence and it arbitrariness were taken for granted and therefore neglected; no one questions or examines what is obvious to all.

From this author's examination of the edition of the *Encyclopedia of Social Work* published in 1977, there was no entry that specifically deals with social work practice in the context of violence except for one on child abuse. There is no mention of the implications of violence on women, the elderly, the disabled or gays or lesbians. In the *1983-84 Supplement to the Encyclopedia*, there is no relevant entry except for Alfred J. Kahn's thoughtful analysis of child and spouse abuse under the entry "Social Issues."

Kahn links the saliency of child and spouse abuse to changes in the structure and function of contemporary families and their social environments which can no longer readily shield or absorb family violence as a major social problem. Government policy and funding began to be directed at alternative approaches to identifying and handling these problems.

Finally in the 1987 edition of the *Encyclopedia of Social Work*, "Victimization Programs and Victims of Crime" became a subject. Self-help groups are mentioned in passing, as a modality.

One of the few areas of interest in social services under the Reagan administration has been programs for victims of crime and domestic violence. On the State and local levels, requirements for mandatory reporting, quick response systems, greater collaboration between police and social agencies, continuous case monitoring and changes in criminal statutes have been instituted to handle incidents of child abuse. In some states there have also been some changes in respect to how cases of spouse abuse and elder abuse are handled.

SOCIAL SERVICES AND CRIME VICTIMS

Within the last fifteen years there has been a burgeoning growth of services directed to crime victims which include monetary compensation, and reimbursed or free counseling and health services to deal with the immediate and longer term consequences of victimization.

Galway and Hudson (1981, 1) wrote,

After centuries of neglect, the crime victim is being discovered. With rediscovery, crime victims have become the object of attention for public policy makers. Social service providers or academics interested in crime victims have been forging the skeleton of a new discipline — "Victimology." In the 1960's several nations and states, primarily in the English-speaking world, moved to establish publicly financed programs or provide victims with financial compensation for medical costs and loss of wages, because of injuries sustained as a result of violent crime.

There has been a quickening of interest in the emerging field of victim services as indicated by the great frequency of social work articles and books on victimization into the 1980s. The newness of victim services has of necessity led to a great deal of experimentation, *ad hoc* programming and successive efforts to determine the nature of victims' needs both in the community and in institutions related to the victimization process.

THE CONTRIBUTION OF GROUP WORK

This publication represents a collection of thoughtful articles which demonstrate the value of social group work concepts applied to domestic and other forms of violence.

Powers' thorough examination of different forms of domestic violence and the appropriate models of social work with groups is a seminal contribution to theory and scholarship. Her article is a superb introduction to the articles that follow which use behavioral, interactional and humanistic approaches toward different service populations.

The ideological underpinnings of group work practice for a violent world find expression in Nosko and Wallace's development of a humanistic and androgynous model of service to male abusing men. Farley and Magill demonstrate how male batterers can benefit from group treatment. Their research effort is an important contribution to emerging areas of practice interest. Of more than passing note are the important contributions being made by our North American colleagues from Toronto and Montreal to group work theory, practice and research in the area of domestic violence.

Sirles and Associates describe creative interventions with victims of childhood sexual abuse. Haran indicates the value of a group in a crisis situation as children in a school become secondary victims or "survivors" of a homicide of a classmate. Sensitivity and creativity are not absent from group work practice with crime victims, and are probably requirements for work with very young victims of violence.

This editor believes that the "sounds of practice" may be as eloquent a teacher as theory, models and research. Xenarios and Seskin, two energetic and passionate social workers, react to their work and give us the voices of rape survivors and battered women. These papers, direct from the world of practice, overwhelm, yet draw us into sympathy and reflection. Not bad stances to consider the horrific consequences of violence that are found all about us.

REFERENCES

Arendt, H. (1969). *On Violence*. New York: Harcourt, Brace Jovanovich.

Encyclopedia of Social Work, Seventeenth Edition (1977). Washington, D.C.: National Association of Social Workers.

Final Report, Attorney General's Task Force on Victims of Crime (1984). Washington, D.C.: U.S. Government Printing Office, September, 1984.

Final Report, President's Task Force on Victims of Crime (1982). Washington, D.C.: U.S. Government Printing Office, December, 1982.

Galaway, B. and Hudson, J. (1981). "Introduction," in *Perspective on Crime Victims* in B. Galaway and J. Hudson (Eds.) St. Louis: C.V. Mosby.

Kahn, A.J. (1984). "Social Trends: Emerging Trends," in the *1984-84 Supplement to the Encyclopedia of Social Work*. Seventeenth Edition. Washington, D.C.: National Association of Social Workers.

Schultz, L.G. (1987). "Victimization Programs and Victims of Crime" in the *Encyclopedia of Social Work, Eighteenth Edition*, 817-22.

Differential Models of Social Work Groups with Family Violence

Roxanne Power

SUMMARY. This paper examines the research literature on multiple forms of family violence and proposes three social work group models to apply to this widespread phenomenon. The models proposed are group work with wife abusers, groups of reciprocated violent marital dyads and multiple violent family unit groups. The theoretical approach of each model is discussed as well as group composition, goals, tasks, structure, relational-interactional systems, worker role and means of service delivery. Important problems in group development of each model are identified and suggestions for worker intervention are outlined.

THE CONCEPT OF FAMILY

Somers defined the family as a ". . . continuous, autonomous group . . . generally recognized as one of the most crucial in maintaining the integrity of the individual and of society" (Hartford, 1971, pp. 25-26). As primary groups families provide personal identity, patterning of sexual roles, social role integration, acceptance of social responsibility and a matrix for affectional bonds (Ackerman, 1958). Functions of the family include satisfaction of affectional needs, protection, upbringing and socialization of children, material maintenance of family members and other subsidiary functions such as political, religious, cultural, ritual, etc. (Howells, 1968).

The family has several unique group characteristics which include a widely diverse age range, intense relationships with a long

Roxanne Power, MSW, is a doctoral student at the University of Toronto, Faculty of Social Work, 246 Bloor Street, West, Toronto, Canada M5S 1A1.

history (Howells, 1968), membership is not contingent on individual behaviour (Hill, 1965; Weick, 1971), involuntary membership (Sprey, 1969), and continuity (Hartford, 1971). Cooley (Lang, 1983) saw the family as a multibonded group with cohesion, permanency, a sense of identity and interdependence amongst members.

The family as a social system has been viewed from several theoretical perspectives. Sprey (1969) felt most clinicians perceive the family as a consensual unit which acts as a buffer between the individual and the larger society. However, Dahrendorf proposed that ". . . like all other institutions the family also may be described as a system of conflict management" (Sprey, 1969, p. 700). Ackerman (1958, p. 19) saw the family as a "kind of exchange unit" with parents acting as the primary contributors. Finally, Goode (1971) viewed the family as a power system where resources of economics, prestige, love or force are used to extract compliance from members.

FORMS AND FREQUENCY OF FAMILY VIOLENCE

Recent recognition of the wide prevalence of family violence has begun to challenge our society's view of the home as a place of nurturance and harmony. Three major theoretical approaches have been proposed to explain this family violence phenomenon. Gelles (1980) noted that the initial, but less supported theory, is the psychiatric model which proposed that intrapsychic reasons (e.g., mental illness, alcohol/drug addiction) caused family violence.

Social-psychological theories which study how the external environment impacts on the family have been presented as the second cause of family violence. Gil (1970) and Straus et al. (1980) found stressful situations had a high correlation to family violence, while Gelles (1974) and Borland (1976) showed social isolation increased the risk of abuse. Socioeconomic status also has been found to affect the level of family violence (Gayford, 1975; Gelles, 1973; Straus et al., 1980).

A third major theoretical approach used to explain family violence is the sociocultural model which studies violence on a societal, rather than individual or family level. Socially structured inequality and cultural norms about violence are factors proposed to perpetuate violence (Dobash and Dobash, 1979; Marsden, 1978). Stark and McEvoy's (1970) study found that one in four men and one in six women felt it was acceptable for a husband to hit a wife under certain conditions, while many parents feel they have the prerogative to physically punish their children (Straus et al., 1980). Gelles (1980) found 5.7% of 1140 families studied had threatened or actually used a weapon on their children at least once while 46.4% had shoved, grabbed or pushed the child.

Although violence can have several definitions for the purposes of this article it will be defined as acts which have a high probability of causing injury to the victim, and include hitting, kicking, shoving, throwing objects and use of weapons (Straus et al., 1980, p. 875). Family violence is exhibited at several interpersonal levels including unilateral or reciprocal spousal violence, parent to child, sibling to sibling, and child to parent abuse (Steinmetz, 1977a; Straus et al., 1980).

The first widely recognized form of family violence was parent to child abuse. The battered child syndrome identified by Kempe et al. (1962) has resulted in legislation which mandates reporting of all suspected cases of child abuse in all areas of Canada and the United States. Straus et al. (1980) in a national study of representative intact families in the United States found 73% of parents reported physical violence toward their children at some time while 63% mentioned at least one violent episode within the twelve month period studied. Mothers more frequently resorted to parental violence and boys were twice as badly beaten child victims (Straus et al., 1980). Abused children are much more likely to become abusive parents (Gil, 1970; Kempe et al., 1962; Straus et al., 1980).

Wife abuse has come to public attention since the seventies decade. England founded the first women's transition home (Pizzey, 1974) and the concept has spread rapidly throughout North America. Health and Welfare Canada (1982) estimated that one in ten women is physically abused. Star (1982) reviewed all existent programs for family violence in the United States and found 110 programs — the majority of which focused on child abuse or wife abuse exclusively.

Although women are not the exclusive victims in spousal violence it is felt that wife abuse deserves more attention because women are more likely to be seriously hurt in domestic violence (Straus et al., 1980) and they are more economically dependent on their husbands and hence less able to escape violent situations (Marsden, 1978). Finally, an important aspect for clinicians wishing to break the cycle of family violence is the findings of Straus et al. (1980) that clearly illustrated abused wives are more likely to abuse their children.

Husband battering is becoming an acknowledged entity in family violence. Wolfgang (1958) found both husbands and wives were equally likely to be slain in domestic violence disputes. Straus et al. (1980) found 49% of the 342 violent family respondents studied had reciprocal marital violence. They also found that in cases of unilateral violence 27% of the husbands and 24% of the wives were physically violent.

Sibling violence, according to Steinmetz (1977c) and Straus et al. (1980), is the most frequent form of family violence. They also found children exposed to or victims of family violence are more likely to engage in sibling violence; however, the frequency of sibling violence decreases in families as the children become older. Later, the abused child exhibits a much higher probability of becoming an abused or abusing spouse and so the cycle of family violence is perpetuated intergenerationally (Gayford, 1978; Straus et al., 1980).

Still another form of family violence much less known is child-to-parent abuse (sometimes referred to as "granny bashing"). Straus et al. (1980) found one in five children (18%) had hit their parent in the twelve-month period studied. They also found that children who were not hit by parents were much less likely to strike their parents.

. The importance of social work intervention in family violence is evident. "Each generation learns to be violent by being a participant in a violent family" (Straus et al., 1980, p. 121). Intervention at the levels of abusive interpersonal relations is necessary to break this circular effect.

This article suggests a group work medium for service delivery in these areas of family violence. Three differential models of social work groups are suggested: (1) group work with wife abusers, (2) group work with reciprocally violent marital dyads, and (3) group work with the multiple violent family unit. For the purposes of this analysis a social work group is defined as a process in which an autonomous group is the central means of service delivery and members develop group goals with the workers, although there is also recognition of meeting individual members' needs (Lang, 1979). The structure of the group should be of a size ". . . small enough for everyone to get around" (Hartford, 1964, p. 234) and the worker's degree of involvement will depend on the group's development stage.

SOCIAL WORK GROUPS WITH WIFE ABUSERS

One of the traditional methods of intervention with family violence is treatment of identified wife abusers through a group work modality. The remedial social work group model appears appropriate for this situation. Vinter (1965) developed this theoretical model to help individuals within a group context. Prevention or rehabilitation are the common goals for the group while individual treatment plans are formulated according to diagnosed need (Papell and Rothman, 1966).

Bertcher and Maple (1974) recommended that commonality of problem and behaviour are more important in group composition than descriptive attributes such as age, socioeconomic status etc. In fact, disparate membership may widen perceptions and enhance the problem-solving function of the group (Gutman, 1983; Tuckman, 1964). Composition in groups for wife abusers would be based on commonality of problem and behaviour. This population is often court mandated, although self-referrals from men fearful of losing their families is also common. Heap (1977) noted that formed or compulsory groups may present an ambivalent or hostile image which the worker should acknowledge openly, while Bertcher and Maple (1974) suggested giving members control over group entry when possible.

The nature of the client in many of these groups may include an absence of self-esteem, fears of dependency or external control, and poor impulse control (Currie, 1983). Many lack the ability to form object relation schema or intimacy with others (L. Bandler, 1967) and their identification system may be undifferentiated (Minuchin et al., 1967). Often these men view the marriage with fixed role expectations (Currie, 1983) and Tuckman (1964) classified this type of personality structure as concrete and undifferentiated. These men use power in decision-making rather than expertise, love or prestige (Goode, 1971).

The limited capacity of these men to differentiate and share, as well as the individualized focus of the group goals, may impede the development of a cohesive social work group formation. Instead the group structure may resemble more a collectivity of individuals. Lang (1979) defined collectivities as time limited, highly structured, with an explicit purpose, and an individual focus with worker predominance in service delivery.

Levinson (1973) classified four types of goals commonly found in groups. These were individual or group goals of a task-instrumental focus or a growth-expressive nature. In this proposed remedial model the individual's goals for individual growth might include improved self-image and ability to communicate on a more intimate level. Achievement of individual instrumental tasks such as anger control might also be addressed.

The major goals in a remedial group for wife abusers should be formulated conjointly by the worker and each individual prior to group commencement and with the knowledge that this process must mediate between the needs of the agency and the client. This is an essential step in the treatment process since the client's commitments to the designated goals will enhance any delivery of group work service (Hartford, 1971) while allowing the client some self-autonomy. At a later date the worker should contract with the group for any goals they may wish to achieve as a whole (e.g., improved parenting skills).

The remedial model's focus, structure, tasks, and goals will determine the relational-interactional nature of the group process. Lang (1983) noted that the hierarchical relationship is dominant in disparately composed groups. The remedial model with the central role of the worker and emphasis on individual goals would necessitate a relational-interactional subsystem of worker-member. However, the worker retains continuous responsibility for all group members and hence an equally important subsystem is worker-group. The skilled group worker would strive to involve the whole group in problem-solving for a particular member's needs, thus a member-worker-group subsystem may emerge.

The worker's role in this group work model, especially in the beginning stages of group formation, would be a directive type common to allonomous groups (Lang, 1972). The worker would function as a change agent or enabler to help the wife abusers alter their conflictual style of interaction.

Since many of these men may lack adequate role models the worker will also be expected to perform this function. Recently Bern and Bern (1984) have advocated male-female team leaders to role model assertive behaviour and conflict resolution between sexes, as well as help the men begin to positively differentiate male-female relationships. Finally, in many groups the worker must role model and provide nurturance. Breton (1979) used this approach with groups of abusing mothers, while S. Bandler (1967) found workers often have to meet the nurturing needs of emotionally developmentally delayed adults before client trust can be gained.

Service delivery to any group of wife abusers will include several common features. Group workers must employ a confrontative and reality-oriented approach since members need to accept responsibility for their violent action (Buckley et al., 1983; Currie, 1983). Thomas (1978) advocated use of behaviour modification in groups: areas of anger control, alcohol reduction etc. may benefit from this intervention. Network building, both between group members and outside agencies is extremely important (Bern and Bern, 1984; Krain, 1982; Martin, 1978). Nurturance and increased self-esteem can be promoted through recurring acceptance of the men as persons, but not their violent behaviour. Constructive conflict resolution can be beneficial in a group setting (Northen, 1969; Shulman, 1967) and can be practiced within this group through the leader's acknowledgement of negative group feelings and subsequent problem-solving.

Vital stages in group development can differ according to group composition, individual development etc. There is one important stage which may be a common component in groups for wife abusers. The problem involves power struggles or unilateral, independent responses of group members. Tuckman (1964) theorized that these behaviours are frequent consequences in groups with concrete, undifferentiated personalities. Additionally, Allen and Straus (1979), Gelles (1982) and Goode (1971) all suggested that wife abusers frequently use coercion (i.e., threats or force) as a means of resolving conflict. The worker must curtail any destructive group power struggles and lay ground rules for constructively resolving differences of opinion, leadership role etc.

Of equal importance is the need for the worker to stress that each member contribute to the group, according to his ability. This individual contribution should produce three consequences. First, it may help the members increase their sense of self-worth. Second, it may aid members to differentiate the uniqueness of each person and third it should encourage a cohesive group formation more representative of a social work group. Feldman (1969a) found functional integration (i.e., regularly performed acts serving the group's needs) aided goal attainment, pattern maintenance and tension management. Later, Feldman (1969b) found group cohesion was increased when group tasks were distributed amongst members, rather than a select few performing all functions.

In sum, the suggested model of group work for wife abusers is a remedial approach. Group composition of undifferentiated, concrete personalities who lack intimacy or object relations schema may evolve as an allonomous collectivity of individuals which requires frequent worker intervention. (See Figure 1.) Dependent on the skill of the worker, individual potential and the duration of the group (e.g., open-ended, brief or long-term duration) the process may reach an autonomous social work group; however, even the collectivity can serve a function of helping members ". . . to stretch their capacity to tolerate difference, find commonality and give acceptance" (Lang, 1983, p. 24).

SOCIAL WORK GROUPS FOR RECIPROCALLY VIOLENT MARITAL DYADS

A form of family violence which appears to have received minimal casework or group work attention is reciprocal violence between marital dyads; however, recent research of intact families showed that this problem deserves immediate attention (Straus et al., 1980).

The group work approach advocated for violent marital dyads most closely resembles the reciprocal model. Schwartz (1971) viewed this theoretical model as a mediating process which stresses the concept of mutual aid; thus the "client" is the group entity. With the use of this model family conflict would be perceived as normal and the mutuality theme of cooperation, rather than violence, would be stressed.

Group composition might originate from family service agencies or couples wishing to improve their marital relationship. Since the couple is wiling to seek help together there may be a degree of dyadic bonding of affection or parenting, thus, members in this group would have some ability to differentiate and engage in limited intimacy. Tuckman (1964) found this type of group composition was capable of a problem-solving approach based on data-processing and use of a consensus model.

A typical client in these groups frequently is unable to resolve conflict in a constructive manner and resorts to violence as the final decision-making mechanism. As well, a lack of effective communication skills may further impede any conciliatory efforts. Some of the sources of conflict may include management of children, monies, sex and affection (Straus et al., 1980) and rigid role expectations (Currie, 1983).

The structure of this group would resemble an autonomous social work group. Goals of the group would precede the needs of the individual; however, since all members would be urged to participate equally in goal setting the group goals should be reflective of the individual needs. The goals might change as the needs of the group emerged more fully.

The common goals would likely be a combination of a group growth and group task nature. A growth goal of the group might include improvement of communication skills through clarification and empathic listening. Likely group task goals might be to learn and apply the steps of conflict resolution, participate in parental education sessions, or impulse control.

The worker role in this group is a facilitator or mediator who enables members to decide mutual goals and ways to achieve these ends (Papell and Rothman, 1966). At times the worker may also need to act as expert or instructor. An especially important function

FIGURE 1

WIFE ABUSERS

Group Population: formed group of men who initiate abuse with marital or sexual partners; voluntary or in-voluntary group attendance

Profile of Members: – concrete or primitive conceptualization
– poor impulse control
– absence of self-esteem
– undifferentiated or rigid role system
– lack ability to share or achieve intimacy
– poor socialization and communication skills

Group Work Approach: Remedial (Vintner, 1965)

Purposes: – to provide nurturance and support
– to promote differentiation initially as group member and later generalization to outside group situations
– to learn impulse control. Initially imposed from worker, then other group members and finally self
– to provide a resocialization process

Focus of Group: Primary focus is on the needs of the individual
                  as formulated conjointly by worker and each
                  member prior to group commencement. Secondary
                  group goals may be contracted with the group
                  as a whole at a later time.

Role of Worker: - directive
                  - accepting of person, not behaviour
                  - role model: nurturance; conflict resolution;
                    assertion
                  - impose controls as needed
                  - function as change agent or enabler
                  - encourage network building among members
                    and outside resources
                  - use of a reality-oriented approach
                  - confrontation, when appropriate

19

of the worker is to role model conflict management amongst members and illustration of good communication skills.

Ideally, the relational-interactional subsystems in this group would focus primarily on a member-group, member-member, or member-dyad level. The worker would retain a fluctuating peripheral interaction with the group becoming more directive or visible when the need arose (Lang, 1972).

The means of service delivery to groups of reciprocally violent spouses include partialization of problems, instruction in and application of conflict resolution, communication feedback, emphasis on the here and now, network building for families, role modelling and educational sessions. The analogy of authority struggles and communication distortion in both groups and families should be stressed.

Simulations of real conflict situations can be role played by the group leaders or the couples themselves. Prior didactic/discussion sessions regarding the theory of conflict resolution should present the couples with guidelines to negotiate actual problem areas. Both the worker and other group members can give direct input into the step by step interaction process evolving and suggestions for alternative solutions. Hopefully, newly developed skills of conflict management and effective communication will be generalized to the dyad's home situation.

One of the most important group processes for reciprocally violent marital dyads will revolve around the issue of power struggles and alliances amongst group members. The group participants are spousal partners who frequently use coercion or position to dictate decision-making. Such members may replicate this practise in the group through formation of alliances for protection or intimidation. To illustrate, a subgroup of men or women with rigid role definitions may feel particularly threatened by the concept of equal decision-making and form coalitions to protect their "territorial domain."

The vital role of the worker in this stage of group development is to ensure discussion emerges about this struggle and to role model the use of conflict management to resolve it. The theme of mutuality and cooperation between dyads and group members must be stressed as the central group goal.

Another potential negative process occurring in these groups may be the tendency of couples to constantly refer to past histories of fighting (Weick, 1971). The worker must assume a directive role and reassert that conflict resolution involves a rational, problem-centred focus with a here and now orientation, rather than an emotional, person-centred approach (Rubin and Brown, 1975).

In summary, the reciprocal model of social work group can be effectively utilized with dyads of reciprocally violent spouses. This group with a more developed sense of identity and differentiation can assume an autonomous status with a fluctuating need for worker intervention. Conflict resolution and communication skills would be the prime interventions role modelled by the worker. (See Figure 2.)

SOCIAL WORK GROUPS WITH THE MULTIPLE VIOLENT FAMILY UNIT

Research has shown that violence can exist in multiple forms in families (Gayford, 1978; Straus et al., 1980; Steinmetz, 1977c). In instances where multiple and repeated forms of family violence exist the family unit may be perceived as a client for group work treatment. Often these client groups will evolve from family service or child welfare agencies as mandatory or voluntary referrals.

The developmental model of social work groups appears the most appropriate theoretical approach for the family unit. Tropp (1976) defined several basic characteristics of this model which readily apply to the family group. First, this approach stresses mutual goals yet there is potential to allow for individual differential gains. This is particularly relevant for families which possess mutual themes, goals and family boundaries, but simultaneously they must recognize the individuality of each member. This model stressing social functioning and the developmental potential of each member appears most adaptable for family intervention.

Second, in developmental group work theory, Tropp (1976) noted peer relationships exist between members. Although family units have broad age ranges, diverse individual interests, and various stages of individual developments there are natural subgroups of peers (i.e., spouses, siblings) as well as formed cross-generations coalitions (e.g., mother-daughters).

FIGURE 2

RECIPROCALLY VIOLENT MARITAL DYADS

Group Population: Formed group of several marital dyads who engage
in reciprocal spousal violence; however, one
spouse may be the more frequent initiator.
Voluntary attendance (although one spouse may
feel coercion by partner to attend)

Profile of Members: - limited ability to abstract
- some ability to differentiate self from others
some dyadic bonding through affection or
parenting
- lack effective communication system
- ineffective, repetitious patterns of problem-
solving
- poor skills of conflict resolution

Group Work Approach: Reciprocal (Schwartz, 1971)

Purposes: - to learn and practice effective communication
skills
- to introduce modes and practice of problem-
solving skills
- to improve impulse control
- to learn and practice steps in conflict
resolution

Focus of Group: The goals of the entire group would receive
                   primary consideration. All dyads would be ex-
                   pected to participate fully in suggesting and
                   reaching consensus on the goals to be accomplished.
                   Goals may change as time passes.

Role of Worker: - some directiveness diminishing as members
                     become an effective group
                   - role model: mediation; nurturance, tolerance
                     of ambiguity regarding spousal or parenting
                     roles; good communication skills and feedback
                   - act as group consultant in problem-solving
                     skills
                   - provide for educational sessions regarding
                     conflict resolution, effective parenting, etc.
                   - demonstrate and encourage active role-playing
                     to practice skills of conflict resolution,
                     communication and problem solving
                   - emphasize reality of here and now

Tropp (1976) noted a third characteristic of developmental groups is their self-direction and autonomy. As a family unit with an open or closed system, this group has developed a decision-making model (albeit a faulty one in violent families) which it utilizes for common problems or crises.

Fourth, the model employs a humanistic theory which values each person's unique contribution to the group. In families members are accepted for themselves and not for how they specifically benefit the group. Although scapegoating may occur in families and other group settings the family member is not usually banished as he might likely be in formed groups. Membership in families is permanent.

Finally, the developmental model uses a specialized approach and thus can recognize the developmental stages and needs of each individual (e.g., adolescent's need for self-autonomy); the developmental phase of family life (e.g., childbearing or "empty nest" syndrome); and the developmental stage in family group work dynamics (e.g., struggle for power and control or differentiation).

The family as a natural group composition has ascribed status, nonvoluntary membership with a wide diversity of age ranges, personalities and interests (Howells, 1968; Sprey, 1969). Dependent on the nature of the membership the violent family unit may be simply a "physical unit" where parents fulfill their duties as a societal obligation only; a "dominated unit" where one member acts as autocratic leader; or a "stable unit" that has permanency but lacks adaptability thus increasing its vulnerability in crisis (Howells, 1968, p. 18). Assessment of family composition is crucial to help the worker determine viable group and individual goals which may be accomplished.

Family units may be exhibiting violence as a response to external pressures, interpersonal difficulties or a crisis situation (Hill, 1965). In such instances, the family structure may regress to an allon-allonomous group (Lang, 1983) and hence the worker may need to assume a more central role for a time-limited period in the initial stages of working with the family (Parad et al., 1976).

However, other families with multiple violence may be in a constant state of conflict, multiproblems and permeating disorganization (L. Bandler, 1967; Minuchin et al., 1967). In some families the parents may be unable to differentiate themselves from their children and the needs of the adults take precedence in these "families of children" (L. Bandler, 1967, p. 231). Ackerman and Behrens defined these family groups as "unintended families" (Howells, 1968, pp. 16-17). The group structure in these family units closely resembles Lang's (1983) definition of a collectivity of individuals and the worker must assume a directive and central role.

The group goals for the family must be formulated in conjunction with the entire family and the social worker. However, the worker will also need to formulate individual goals with each member or subgroup according to their needs. The worker, for example may contract with the parental subgroup to enable them to improve parental or conflict management skills, while the adolescent may need help to negotiate more power in decision-making. Dependent on the functioning autonomy of the family the worker may need to take a more participative role in realistic and appropriate goal setting.

The tasks in work with family units will involve a combination of both group and individual goals with growth and task focus. Group expressive-growth goals might include improved family communication, especially in the areas of affection, while an appropriate group task goal might involve helping family members develop a daily routine of chores. Recognition of individual goals is also important in working with families. Individual growth goals might include an adolescent's ease in positively projecting himself as a person separate from his family, while an individual task goal might be developing choices for a career option.

The relational interactional subsystems in the family unit are diverse. In the allon-autonomous family the main relational interactions may be on member-member, member-group or member-subgroup levels with the worker facilitating or mediating interactions as needed. However, in the allonomous "family collectivity" meaningful relational interactions initially may be primarily between worker-member, worker-subgroup or worker-group. The worker may need to gain individual trust from members before group cohesion can occur. Levine (1965) identified a similar progression of relational interactions which occurred when mental health social workers began to work in the home environment with low income, multiproblem families.

The worker role with autonomous or allon-autonomous family groups will be a facilitator-mediator position allowing individual members and the family unit to develop their full potential. Role modelling or discussion of appropriate adult, parental, child and spousal roles may be an important function of the worker. Additionally in the allonomous group, the worker must be prepared to act as expert and teacher (S. Bandler, 1967) as well as providing nurturance (Breton, 1979) and frequent positive feedback to both the parents and children.

The means of group service delivery to family units with multiple violence includes emphasis on the here and now, and expansion of coping mechanisms through problem-solving skills, support systems and delayed gratification. Conflict management techniques should be stressed and a model of family decision-making agreeable to all members should be developed. The worker, stressing a mutuality theme, helps the family become a true social work group by helping members to selectively subordinate their individual needs to those of the family entity. (See Figure 3.)

Thus families exhibiting multiple violence, either as a consequence of crisis or chaotic lifestyle, should be worked with as a whole system within a social work group framework. The primary goal is ". . . co-operation through a set of shared, mutually understood procedural rules" (Sprey, 1969, p. 703). The worker aids the group's development of these conflict management skills with the hope that a change in behaviour will activate a secondary goal of relationship enhancement (e.g., differentiation, nurturance).

Although this model of group work does have elements of a preventive or remedial approach the developmental group work theory is stressed to enable: (1) development of the potential in family group functioning rather than concentration on the dysfunctional or "bad" behaviour, (2) encourage recognition of the differential identities and needs of individual family members, and (3) enhancement of development in three distinct areas, namely, developmental stage of the family social work group, emotional development of the individual and development of family behaviour appropriate to the family life phase.

FIGURE 3

MULTIPLE VIOLENT FAMILY UNIT

Group Population: Natural group of one nuclear or extended family
unit; several levels of interpersonal violence
which may include spousal, parent to child,
sibling to sibling, etc. Voluntary or mandated
referrals.

Profile of Member: – family members' roles of an undifferentiated,
fluctuating or rigid nature
– no recognition of individual need according
to chronological age and stage of life
– poor parental skills
– chaotic homelife
– little sense of family unity

Group Work Approach: Developmental (Tropp, 1976)

Purposes: – to help family gain a sense of mutuality
and differentiation
– to help improve family decision-making with
appropriate input from all
– to improve parental skills
– to promote communication and interaction
amongst family members

FIGURE 3 (continued)

Focus of Group: Group goals focusing on the needs of a family unit are formulated in conjunction with the worker. However, the worker should help de-fine needs of a family individual or subgroup since often these needs are affecting family functioning directly or indirectly

Role of Worker: - degree of directiveness depends on state of conflict and disorganization existing within family. In very chaotic families the worker may first assume a pseudo-parental role for both parents and children
- role model: nurturance; recognition of different roles and stages of development in both an individual and a family's life; co-operation
- actively promote communication between and across all generational boundaries in the family
- help develop structure and continuity in daily living
- encourage a conflict resolution approach
- active participation in family discussion and recreation in the home setting

REFERENCES

Ackerman, N. (1958) *The psychodynamics of family life*. New York: Basic Books pp. 15-25.

Allen, C. and Straus, M. (1979) Resources, power, and husband-wife violence. In M. Straus and G. Hotaling (Ed.) *The social causes of husband-wife violence*. (Ch. 12) Minneapolis: University of Minnesota Press.

Bandler, L. (1967) Family functioning: A psychosocial perspective. In E. Pavenstedt (Ed.) *The drifters: Children of disorganized lower class families*. (pp. 225-253) Boston: Little, Brown and Co.

Bandler, S. (1967) Casework: A process of socialization. In E. Pavenstedt (Ed.) *The drifters: Children of disorganized lower class families*. (pp. 255-296) Boston: Little, Brown and Co.

Bern, E. and Bern, L. (1984) A group program for men who commit violence against their wives. *Social work with groups 7* (1) 45-62.

Bertcher, H. and Maple, F. (1974) Elements and issues in group composition. In P. Glasser, R. Sarri and R. Vinter (Ed.) *Individual change through small groups*. (pp. 186-208) New York: Free Press.

Borland, M. (1976) (Ed.) *Violence in the family*. Manchester, England: Manchester University Press.

Breton, M. (1979) Helping abusive families through the use of small groups. In S. Abels and P. Abels (Ed.) *Social work with groups: Proceedings 1979 symposium*. (pp. 241-253) Kentucky: Committee for the Advancement of Social Work with Groups.

Buckley, L., Miller, D. and Rolfe, T. (1983) Treatment groups for violent men: A Windsor model. *Social work with groups 6* (3/4) 189-195.

Currie, D. (1983) Treatment groups for violent men: The Toronto approach. *Social work with groups 6* (3/4) 179-188.

Dobash, R.E. and Dobash, R. (1979) *Violence against wives*. New York: Free Press.

Feldman, R. (1969a) Group integration and intense interpersonal disliking. *Human relations 22* (5) 405-413.

Feldman, R. (1969b) Integration, intense interpersonal dislike and social group work intervention. *Social work 14* (3) 30-39.

Gayford, J. (1978) Battered wives. In J. Martin (Ed.) *Violence and the family*. (pp. 19-39) Chichester, England: John Wiley and Sons.

Gelles, R. (1973) Child abuse as psychopathology: A sociological critique and reformation. *American journal of orthopsychiatry 43* (July) 611-621.

_____. (1974) *The violent home: A study of physical aggression between husbands and wives*. Beverly Hills, California: Sage Publications.

_____. (1980) Violence in the family: A review of research in the seventies. *Journal of marriage and family 42* (4) 873-885.

_____. (1982) Applying research on family violence to clinical practice. *Journal of marriage and family 44* (February) 9-20.

Gil, D. (1970) *Violence against children: Physical child abuse in the United States*. Cambridge, Massachusetts: Harvard University Press.

Goode, W. (1971) Force and violence in the family. *Journal of marriage and family 33* (4) 624-636.

Gutman, B. (1983) A proposed model for an adolescent-adult group: The use of disparately composed groups for social work practice. In N. Lang and C. Marshall (Ed.) *Patterns in the mosaic, proceedings, 1982*. (pp. 1014-1030) Toronto: University of Toronto Press.

Hartford, M. (1964) Use of social group work in helping members accept differences. *Social Work Practice*, 1964. NCSW (pp. 220-235) New York: Columbia University Press.

Hartford, M. (1971) Groups in social work. New York: Columbia University Press.

Health and Welfare Canada (1982) Wife battering: A national concern. (Pamphlet.)

Heap, K. (1977) *Group theory for social workers: An introduction*. Oxford: Pergamon Press.

Hill, R. (1965) Generic features of families under stress. In H. Parad (Ed.) *Crisis intervention*. (pp. 32-52) New York: Family Service Association of America.

Howells, J. (1968) Dimensions of the family. In J. Howells (Ed.) *Theory and practice of family psychiatry*. (pp. 9-56) Edinburgh: Oliver and Boyd Ltd.

Kempe, C. et al. (1962) The battered child syndrome. *Journal of American Medical Association 181* (July) 17-24.

Krain, M. (1982) A sociological perspective on the control of violence in families. In J. Flarizen (Ed.) *Many faces of family violence*. (pp. 66-77) Springfield, Illinois: Charles C Thomas.

Lang, N. (1972) A broad-large model of practice in the social work group. *Social service review 46* (1) 76-89.

_____. (1979) Some defining characteristics of the social work group: Unique social form. In S. Abels and P. Abels (Ed.) *Social work with groups: Proceedings 1979 symposium*. (pp. 30-50) Kentucky: Committee for the Advancement of Social Work with Groups.

_____. (1983) Social work practice in small social forms: Some unacknowledged entities. In N. Goroff (Ed.) *Reaping from the field, proceedings, 1981*. (pp. 1-20) Hebron, Connecticut: Practitioner's Press.

Levinson, H. (1973) Use and misuse of groups. *Social work 18* (1) 66-73.

Levine, R. (1965) Treatment in the home. In E. Younghusband (Ed.) *Social work with families*. (pp. 56-70) London: George Allen and Unwin Ltd.

Marsden, D. (1978) Sociological perspectives on family violence. In J. Martin (Ed.) *Violence and the family*. (pp. 103-133) Chichester, England: John Wiley and Sons.

Martin, J. (1978) Some reflections on violence and the family. In J. Martin (Ed.) *Violence and the family*. (pp. 345-352) Chichester, England: John Wiley and Sons.

Minuchin, S. et al. (1967) *Families of the slums*. (pp. 192-243) New York: Basic Books, Inc.

Northen, H. (1969) *Social work with groups*. New York: Columbia University Press.

Papell, C. and Rothman, B. (1966) Social group work models: Possession and heritage. *Education for social work 11* (Fall) 66-77.

Parad, H., Selby, L. and Quinlan, J. (1976) Crisis intervention with families. In R. Roberts and H. Norther (Ed.) *Theories of social work with groups*. (pp. 304-330) New York: Columbia University Press.

Pizzey, E. (1974) *Scream quietly or the neighbours will hear*. London: Penguin Books.

Rubin, J. and Brown, B. (1975) *Social psychology of bargaining and negotiation*. New York: Academic Press.

Schwartz, W. (1971) Social group work: The interactionist approach. In R. Morris (Ed.) *Encyclopedia of social work XVI*. (pp. 1252-63) New York: National Association of Social Workers.

Shulman, L. (1967) Scapegoats, workers and pre-emptive intervention. *Social work 12* (2) 37-43.

Sprey, J. (1969) The family as a system in conflict. *Journal of marriage and family 31* (4) 699-706.

Star, B. (1982) Programs for assaulters. In J. Flanzer (Ed.) *Many faces of family violence*. (pp. 76-86) Springfield, Illinois: Charles C Thomas.

Stark, R. and McEvoy, J. (1970) Middle class violence. *Psychology today 4* (November) 52-65.

Steinmetz, S. (1977a) The use of force for resolving family conflict: The training ground for abuse. *The family coordinator 26* (January) 19-26.

Steinmetz, S. (1977c) *The cycle of violence: Assertive, aggressive and abusive behaviour*. New York: Praeger Publishers.

Straus, M., Gelles, R. and Steinmetz, S. (1980) *Behind closed doors: Violence in the American family*. Garden City, New York: Anchor Press/Doubleday.

Thomas, E. (1971) Social casework and social group work: The behavioural modification approach. In R. Morris (Ed.) *Encyclopedia of social work XVI*. (pp. 1226-1237) New York: National Association of Social Workers.

Tropp, E. (1976) Social group work: The developmental approach. In R. Morris (Ed.) *Encyclopedia of Social Work XVI*. (pp. 1246-1252) New York: National Association of Social Workers.

Tuckman, B. (1964) Personality structure, group composition and group functioning. *Sociometry 27* 469-487.

Vinter, R. (1965) Social group work. In H. Lurie (Ed.) *Encyclopedia of social work XV*. (pp. 715-723) New York: National Association of Social Workers.

Weick, K. (1971) Group processes, family processes and problem solving. In J. Aldous (Ed.) *Family problem-solving*. (pp. 3-39) Illinois: Dryden Press, Inc.

Wolfgang, M. (1958) *Patterns in criminal homicide*. New York: John Wiley and Sons.

Group Work with Abusive Men:
A Multidimensional Model

Anna Nosko
Bob Wallace

SUMMARY. The authors argue that existing models and programs for working with abusive men have been too focussed on strategies of cognitive restructuring. They attempt to expand the understanding of what causes changes by developing a model which places group work theory at the heart of the change process. They illustrate the power of this theoretical perspective by integrating with it psychodynamic, cognitive and sociopolitical theory in a multidimensional model. What emerges is a new model which reconceptualizes male violence and its treatment.

Treatment groups for male batterers owe their genesis to Anne Ganley's work with veterans in the mid-1970s. Although not a theoretical focus of her work, Ganley clearly held that group process was a central variable in effecting behavioural change. Since her pioneering work, however, this dimension to group work with male abusers has largely been lost with the growing preoccupation with cognitive theory. This shift essentially represents the masculinization of the field. Not only has cognitive restructuring become the panacea of change, but the traditionally feminine concern with the dynamics of relationship and with the affective realm has been lost. It is our belief that this shift represents an abandonment of basic social work values and a capitulation to the masculine ethics which we feel to be related to the phenomenon of male violence. It is our goal to attempt a reintegration of cognition, affect, behaviour and

Anna Nosko, MSW, and Bob Wallace, MA, MSW, are Social Workers, Family Services Association of Toronto (West Region), and have collaborated in providing group service to male abusers since January 1984.

33

process into an essentially androgynous model which redefines at the social and intrapsychic levels masculine behaviour. Within this article, androgyny is defined as the midpoint between and integration of the two polarities, the masculine represented by instrumentality and aggression; the feminine represented by emotionality, passive behaviour and a concern with relationships. In order to achieve this we will begin with a brief review of the literature, develop a psychodynamic/cognitive model of intrapsychic process and demonstrate how group process is central to the effectiveness of cognitive-behavioural interventions. In other words, we seek to integrate three theoretical perspectives to produce a multidimensional view of the genesis and treatment of male violence.

THE LITERATURE

In his review of the literature, Gondolf identifies three different theoretical approaches to understanding the male abuser: the psychoanalytic, social learning and sociopolitical theories (Gondolf, 1985). These approaches are generally presumed in the field to be mutually exclusive. In fact, however, each is dealing with different dimensions of human behaviour ranging from the intrapsychic to the macroscopic. Thus, there is no necessary contradiction between them. Nevertheless, treatment theory emerges primarily from social learning theory in that it focuses on reteaching behaviour through cognitive interventions: what is learned in the family of origin can be unlearned. The consequence is that the insights derived from other theory bases is lost in treatment.

The result is a one dimensional intervention that fails to recognize fully the affective and political processes inherent in role negotiation. This is evident in greater or lesser degrees in most models currently being developed (Gondolf, 1985; Edelson, 1984; Saunders, 1984; Currie, 1982, 1986; Neidig and Friedman, 1984; Pressman, 1984; Deschner, 1984, 1986; Taylor, 1984; Bern and Bern, 1984; Weidman, 1986). None fully addresses the importance of the process inherent in groups which facilitates and acts as a crucible of change. Rather, the focus rests almost solely on the use of various strategies of cognitive restructuring. Lacking the recognition of the context of treatment, there is little justification for the use of groups as the primary treatment modality. Indeed, the term group itself, has been corrupted and rendered meaningless. Of writers in this area, Brissan (1982), Bernard and Bernard (1984), Ganley (1981) and Deschner (1986) begin to explore and acknowledge the power of group with this population. None, however, addresses group process as a primary instrument of change. Heppner (1981), Gold (1981), and Stein (1983) stress the importance of social work group work with men in general; however, this entire body of theory has been split off from an understanding of what effects change in male abusers.

Another problem is that up until now there has been little empirical resource to substantiate the assumptions upon which an entire treatment approach is based. Although some outcome studies have been done, e.g., Neidig and Freedman (1984), there is no clear relationship evident between outcome and intervention. Nevertheless, it is assumed that outcome is a product of cognitive interventions alone, and yet our own experience in working with these men for two years is that the men themselves identify the group process as effecting the greatest amount of change in their view of themselves.

Tragically, the focus of treatment has begun to define the focus of research. The danger is great that the questions which will guide research efforts will bypass completely what is, perhaps, the most effective vehicle for effecting change—the group. Should this happen, validity for group as a treatment modality will be lacking. Group may then become a peripheral part of the treatment process and the full definition of group may become bastardized further.

A grouping has been interchanged with the concept of building a mature group (Lang, 1981) in which the affective and social dimensions of change are seen as central in effecting individual change. In part, this reflects the difficulty in operationally defining concepts such as group process.

DYNAMICS OF THE MALE ABUSER

Having considered some of the germane problems within the literature as a whole, it is necessary to begin the process of integrating social group work theory and intrapsychic process. We will begin by explaining the latter.

It is our basic belief that human behaviour is the product of an interaction between emotion, cognition and the ego ideal which is rooted in an internalization of external socialization processes. The range of permissible affect is determined by the self-concept and is expressed within the context of implicit societal norms. This view represents a traditional psychodynamic model of human behaviour and is useful in pulling together into one coherent picture some of the characteristics of abusive men identified in the literature. Specifically, it is assumed that violent men adhere to rigid role structures (Pressman, 1984; Harris and Sinclair, 1981; Walker, 1979), poor impulse control (Pressman, 1984; Cantoni, 1984; Harris and Sinclair, 1981; Star, 1980; Bernard and Bernard, 1984), strong dependency needs (Harris and Sinclair, 1981; Cantoni, 1984; Pressman 1984; Bernard and Bernard, 1984), and a limited range of affect (Gondolf, 1985; Sinclair, 1985; Ganley, 1981). In addition, they tend to be socially isolated (Sinclair, 1985; Bernard and Bernard, 1984; Ganley, 1981) and tend to view their wives as possessions (Star, 1980; Bernard and Bernard, 1984; Walker, 1979; Pressman, 1984). Finally, they are seen to resort to denial and externalization of responsibility for their violence (Harris and Sinclair, 1981; Pressman, 1984; Star, 1980; Bernard and Bernard, 1984; Purdy and Nickle, 1981; Walker, 1979).

It is interesting to compare what is considered to be a profile of abusive men with the social characteristics ascribed to men in general. In his summary of the literature on common male concerns, Heppner includes the following: achievement, power and control, competition, restrictive emotionality, homophobia, sexual and career performance, interpersonal relationships, coping with changing male and female sex roles, and intimacy (Heppner, 1981).

Goldberg sees traditional masculinity in similar terms: "The male has become anaesthetized and robotized because he has been heavily socialized to repress and deny almost the total range of his emotions and human needs in order that he can perform in the acceptable 'masculine' way" (Goldberg, 1976). Goldberg later suggests that this leads to a compulsive need to prove masculine identity in what he terms "macho-psychotic behaviour" (Goldberg, 1979). Similar themes are echoed by Tolson (1977), Hoch (1979), Gondolf (1985), and Neidig and Friedman (1984).

It is our supposition, then, that violent men share with traditional men, in general, an ego ideal which values aggression and power over others and which denies permission to experience a broad range of ego dystonic "Feminine" emotions. The consequence is a variety of defense mechanisms which are designed both to preserve the abuser's concept of self as masculine and to ensure socially sanctioned behaviours. Thus, the abuse is defending against a perception of self as inadequate or Feminine as well as the affect associated with such a view of self. By controlling their wives through violent behaviour, they are therefore, able to experience themselves as powerful. This view is similar to that of Gondolf who sees the abuser's self-esteem as dependent on excessive internal and external control (Gondolf, 1985).

The primary defense mechanisms used by the abuser include denial and minimization of the violence (Dutton, 1986; Harris and Sinclair, 1981; Sinclair, 1985; Currie, 1985; Star, 1980; Walker, 1979; Bernard and Bernard 1984; Neidig and Friedman, 1984), splitting, projection (Neidig and Friedman, 1984), repressions (Neidig and Friedman, 1984) and intellectualization. Of particular importance are denial and minimization of the violence: unless these defenses are punctured by a precipitating crisis and by treatment, no motivation is available as leverage to effect change.

Splitting and projection are also central to the dynamics of abuse. It is our supposition that ego dystonic dependency needs and "Feminine" emotions are split off and projected onto their wives in a process of projective identification. This is similar to the argument advanced by Weitzman and Dreen that abusive relationships often involve a high degree of enmeshment (Weitzman and Dreen, 1982).

This does not mean, however, that the spouse participates in any responsibility for the violence. It simply means that any given relationship resonates with the needs of the individuals in it. The woman's needs do not include a need to be abused. As Cantoni (Cantoni, 1981), Walker (Walker, 1979), and a host of others point out, women who stay in abusive relationships do so for a variety of reasons that have nothing to do with a need for or an acceptance of the violence.

One of the consequences of these defense mechanisms is the need to convert a broad range of "unmasculine" emotion into the masculine affect, anger. This is the funnelling effect described by Gondolf

(Gondolf, 1985) and Ganley (Ganley, 1981). The implication of this is that in many respects anger functions as a defence mechanism. This represents a shift away from psychodynamic theory which defines anger as an instinct based primary emotion. Cognitive theory, however, provides a useful way of conceptualizing this conversion process. It further provides the point of interface between the intrapsychic and the interpersonal-environmental. In other words, it defines and clarifies the ego based process of mediating between unconscious drive, superego and the environment.

Within cognitive theory, emotion is the consequence of the intellectual appraisal of an actualizing event (Novaco, 1982; Neidig and Freidman, 1984; Beck, 1976; Burns, 1980; Gondolf, 1985). Anger specifically involves the perception that the actualizing event is threatening and dangerous (Novaco, 1982). Any stimulus, whether internal or external, which threatens the masculine ego ideal generates an arousal reaction which is labelled and experienced as anger (Gondolf, 1985). This conforms to the response theory of emotions which argues that emotions are consequent to the interpretation given to internal sensations (Christensen and Pass, 1983). Thus, the experience of ego dystonic emotions (e.g., sadness, hurt, disappointment, shame, humiliation, fear) or conditions (e.g., dependency) can generate an angry response. The more rigid the ego ideal, the greater the perceived threat and the more intense the reaction of anger. Anger, then, manifests in many forms of behaviour ranging from the nonviolent to the violent.

This is necessarily accomplished through a male-female co-leadership which redefines at an experiential level male-female interaction. In this way there is an immediate expansion of the societal baseline from which the individual's ego ideal is generated. In brief, the social work group begins to address the internal and social factors influencing both the cognitive and affective dimensions which are the crucial points of change. This is accomplished by the social work group process which serves as a new microsociety with its own set of curative norms and values. In this context, common external supports to the internal experience of anger and violence can be temporarily suspended. This allows for a reduction of cognitive distortion as well as a reduction for the need for dysfunctional defenses. In turn, an opportunity to relearn and redefine the masculine role emerges. This is in part accomplished by the positive reframing and experience of emotions previously perceived as ego dystonic and threatening. They can now be experienced because the group process is structured by the coleaders in such a way that certain humanistic and androgynous values and norms (e.g., equal access, equal status, nonjudgment) form a baseline which enhances positive and nurturing interactions among members. In turn, a broader experience of the masculine ego ideal is permitted and experienced. This reinforces the validity of the alternative world view which originates with the cotherapists. The entire process therefore becomes self-reinforcing on all levels, i.e., the social, the interpersonal, the cognitive, the affective and the behavioural. An essential but secondary component is the provision, through cognitive interventions, of anger management and nonviolent communications skills. Thus group process is the central vehicle empowering cognitive-behavioural interventions. This analysis is at the core of the model which we have developed over the past two years in our work with male abusers in Toronto. This model finds its basis in the cognitive behavioural programs previously identified but expands the parameters of treatment by integrating social work group therapy.

Where these external forces provide a consistent and positive reinforcement of violent behaviour, the violence is sustained. However, when one or more of the above systems strongly repudiates the behaviour, e.g., the wife leaves, charges are laid, the individual's defense system and cognitive appraisal of the violence are confronted. The power of this confrontation depends on the system or systems involved and the weighting given to them by the individual. Dissonance is, therefore, generated and the abuse is frequently thrown into crisis. Characterized by a broad range of affect previously experienced as anger (e.g., fear of the legal system or loss of wife, despair, shame and guilt). Intervention at this point needs to heighten the cognitive dissonance by reframing the experienced affect as consistent with masculine identity as redefined by the therapist. For example, crying can be reframed as an act of courage and strength which provides a positive definition of the affect and behaviour within the context of other traditional male values. Thus begins the work of reducing the necessity for rigid and dysfunctional defenses. In addition, motivation for entering treatment is enhanced by the positive regard the client experiences and by the further reduction of the need to deny and/or minimize the violence. At the same time, however, there is a risk that the increased experience of affect will generate suicidal ideation and behaviour (Ganley, 1981). The therapist, therefore, needs to maintain a balance between an intensification of affect and the defenses needed to prevent suicidal behaviour. The client must also be apprised of and encouraged to use all available social support networks should the crisis become insupportable to him. Given this view, it is essential in treatment to accomplish four objectives:

1. redefine the masculine ego ideal;
2. validate and help to relabel affect marked by anger;
3. provide a context which supports a new, more comprehensive set of norms and values consistent with a more androgynous view of masculinity;
4. provide the social and interpersonal skills needed to express anger appropriately when it does arise.

The context and means by which the above objectives are accomplished is the closed ended social work group which addresses the cognitive, affective, behavioural and social dimensions of human reality.

In order to develop a more comprehensive view of why anger results in violence in some men but not others, it is necessary to consider both social learning theory and sociopolitical cultural theory which shapes the internal ego ideal, define the range of social skills available to the man, and prescribe the socially acceptable range of behaviours associated with anger. Given the general social approval male violence is given in the media and the political culture as a whole, violence, when it does erupt, is frequently supported by the social systems with which the individual abuser comes into contact. These values, already internalized in the form of the ego ideal, are available to the abuser as a further rationalization of his behaviour and support the defenses of denial, minimization, and projection of responsibility. Social norms are particularly potent for those men who witnessed or were victims of violence in their families of origin. Various studies show that as many as 80% of abusers fall into this category (Gondolf, 1985). Thus, experience in family of origin is not only internalized and seen as consistent with masculine behaviour, but provides the men with a restricted repertoire of behavioural and social skills which equate intense anger with violent behaviours. This leads to a systemic view of the social factors involved in supporting both the defense structures by which these men justify or excuse their violence and which sanction male violence in and of itself. Specifically, violence is supported by five major subsystems:

1. institutions of male and female socialization, e.g., the family of origin, work where the competitive ethic demands repression of feeling (Hoch, 1977), the media and advertising;
2. legal system, i.e., the failure to lay charges, delays in court hearings, conviction with insignificant sentence;
3. personal network, i.e., peers and family who normalize the violence and urge the woman to stay;
4. social delivery system, e.g., the helping professions' use of an interactional approach which tends to equalize responsibility for the violence (Bograd, 1984) or use of psychoanalytic theory which associates the violence with women's assumed masochism;
5. the spousal response for the violence, i.e., the message conveyed, i.e., the acceptability of violence if the wife stays whatever her reasons.

THE MODEL

We will begin by elaborating more fully the social work group within which cognitive, affective, and behavioural change takes place. The social work group (from now on referred to as the group) comes with its implicit *objectives*, i.e., democratic mutual aid system and actualizing purpose (Papell and Rothman, 1980), *values and norms*, e.g., nonjudgment, egalitarianism, mutual respect, concern and support, open flexible role system, equal status, tolerance for difference, open communication (Lang, 1981), and *structure* designed to empower the group-as-a-whole (Wilson and Ryland, 1980) through, e.g., professional auspice or designated leadership which generates and enforces the above-mentioned features, creating a "micro" society or social system (Klein, 1970) with its internal support system. The objectives, values, norms and structure develop through stages or phases growing towards group maturity (Lang, 1981). It is at this point that changes in the group members are integrated and internalized.

With the internalization of the group norms and values, structure and purpose, the need for rigid defenses diminishes and thus the men are allowed greater access to previously repressed emotions. This allows for a relabelling of their emotions and an expansion of their affective and behavioural repertoire within a humanistic and more androgynous context. This constitutes a recapitulation of their earlier affective and behaviour set (Yalom, 1975) which reduces the need to experience most emotions as anger and removes some of the precursors of violent behaviour. Those elements of self which were previously inconsistent with their masculine self-concept and were split off are integrated because the group has rendered these defenses unacceptable within the "society of the group." The cognitive and behaviour interventions complete this process by providing the necessary interpersonal skill required (and lacking in these men) to express anger in a nonviolent way when it does arise.

LEADERSHIP

Within groups for abusive men the nature of the leadership is of particular importance (Gold, 1981; Purdy and Nickle, 1981; Heppner, 1981; Edelson, 1984). In social work groups in particular it is the leaders' responsibility to deliberately structure the group in such a way that the traditional social group work norms and values hold sway (Lang, 1979).

These more androgynous values themselves are a contradiction of traditional male norms around competitiveness, status and power. This has implications for the power and control phase in the total group process because it is introducing a powerful dissonance.

Of special importance for these groups is the need to use male, female coleaders (Purdy and Nickle, 1981; Bern and Bern, 1984; Stein, 1983) in order to confront the members' belief that masculine and feminine represent absolute polarities. This requires a deliberate use of self on the part of both coleaders: through their interaction the above dissonance is extended to encompass perceptions of male-female interactions. This requires the group workers modelling more androgynous roles. For example, it is necessary that the leaders do not mirror the traditional assignment of affective and interpersonal issues to women and cognitive processes to men (Bern and Bern, 1984). The further implication for the coleaders themselves is a need to heighten personal awareness and resolution of internal gender conflicts (Gold, 1981). The coleaders must, therefore, consciously and deliberately alternate in the handling of various group leadership tasks.

Just as group norms themselves have implications for power and control, so too does the deliberate modelling of alternative male/female roles and interactions. By behaving in unanticipated but deliberate ways, the coleaders will confront very directly the projections, the split off parts of self that group members initially bring into the group. For example, the male leader's demonstration of nonaggressive ways of handling anger in role-plays may lead to an attempt to discredit his behaviours through labelling him "wimpish." Conversely assertive behaviour on the part of the female will be interpreted as "bitchiness." The coleaders must be prepared for such responses and have available to them a strategy for resolving the dissonance thus introduced in the desired direction of androgyny. This again reinforces the need for the coleaders themselves to identify and feel comfortable with androgynous roles (Bern and Bern, 1984).

STAGES OF GROUP PROCESS

Of primary importance in this model is the fact that group process develops through stages towards maturity (Glassman and Kates, 1986). Central to this thesis is the belief that the group is greater than the sum of its parts. In other words the group is an entity unto itself or a micro society whose specified norms and values validate and require the full range of human experience, including those parts of self which are considered by the men to be ego distonic. Enfolding of group process, therefore, reflects the internal struggle through which these men pass on the way to embracing the image of humanity represented by the group. Thus in the passage towards the stage of group maturity, there is a growing identification with the image of self that is upheld by the group as a whole. Given the degree to which this population of men split off and project unmasculine behaviours and emotions, the powers and control stage which precedes intimacy and then differentiation (or maturity) (Garland, Jones and Kolodny, 1973) may be prolonged and intensified because it is at this point that the group members confront most directly their defense structures. The conflict between group and internal defenses is resolved through the modelling effect of the coleaders' androgynous behaviour and through the positive impact of mutual support at a time when these men are feeling highly vulnerable because of the crisis through which they are just passing. Thus the cognitive restructuring around issues of gender identity and role expectations is accomplished more through the emotional climate provided by the group as a micro society than through the didactic content around male socialization that is introduced into the group at various points in its development (Heppner, 1981; Stein, 1983).

We will now consider the issues and intervention characteristics of each stage of group process according to Garland, Jones and Kolodny (1973) with the Preparatory phase coming from Northen (1969).

PREPARATORY STAGE

In developing the group composition, the norms and values of the group are introduced and modelled by the group worker in the screening interviews (Northen, 1969) with each potential group member. The external crisis which provided the initial impetus to receiving treatment provides the opportunity to the worker to heighten the cognitive dissonance and introduce the different value base which will later be developed in group.

The specific worker interventions include the following:

1. drawing a distinction between individual worth and behaviour while at the same time confronting denial and minimization of the violence indirectly by having the client review in as much detail as possible his behaviours during the, at least, last two incidents;
2. giving the client permission to feel and validating the ego distonic emotions aroused by the crisis by exploring the affect and reframing it in such a way that it becomes compatible with a broader definition of masculinity;
3. modelling androgynous behaviours by demonstrating empathy and positive regard and a negative judgement of the violent behaviour.

In this phase contraindication to group treatment are assessed and include the following:

- primary alcohol or drug addiction,
- severe personality disorder (e.g., sociopath, paranoid, borderline disorders),
- psychotic disorders,
- organic brain dysfunction,
- developmental handicap.

PRE-AFFILIATION

In this stage the main dynamics are the safety of each individual, the approach and avoidance dilemma for each individual and a general exploration of the group program. It is important for the group leader(s) to focus on allowing and supporting distance, inviting trust and providing program structure (Garland, Jones and Kolodny, 1973). The deliberate leadership has two goals in mind: to lay the ground for group building and secondly to introduce an alternative model of male/female behaviour and interaction. The didactic/cognitive interventions identified in the literature are particularly useful in this phase because they are least threatening to the individual men while at the same time providing a context for beginning to share at a more intimate affective level. It also provides some immediate skills for handling their anger in a nonviolent way.

The following cognitive behaviour interventions are introduced:

— Identification of Anger Cue,
— Time-Out,
— Self-Talk.

The following group work interventions are introduced:

— modelling by the group leaders,
— supportive confrontations of behaviour,
— role negotiation,
— conflict resolution,
— explicit norm setting,
— contracting, written and verbal,
— inviting participation,
— eliciting individual content to expand upon cognitive behavioural material,
— encouraging limited self-disclosure,
— validating limited expression of affect,
— check-in.

POWER AND CONTROL

Some of the aspects of this stage have previously been discussed. However, it is important to state that it is a crucial phase that if not completed correctly, will lead to the dissolution of the group. The leadership needs to ride the wave of rebelliousness which challenges the norms, values and authority of the leaders. This is a particularly stressful time for both the leaders and the group members. It is the phase within which the power struggle needs to reach clarification. The group members are going through a transition where three issues prevail: (i) rebellion vs. autonomy, (ii) permission and the normative crisis-establishing norms that are the group's vs. the individual's, and (iii) protection and support (Garland, Jones and Kolodny, 1973). It is also the phase in which the leaders will be most subject to the projections of group members. The movement through this phase leads to the beginnings of group cohesiveness. However, it is important to anticipate movement back and forth between the stages of intimacy and power and control.

In passing through this turbulent phase the group members accept and begin to internalize the norms and values of group thus enabling the grouping of individuals to move toward a group as-a-whole. While group members norm and storm, each individual is paralleling this process internally. It is in ending this phase that the group members begin to relinquish both dysfunctional defenses and cognitive distortions. Dealing supportively with affect is, therefore, critical in this stage. The cognitive/behavioural interventions introduced from the previous stage are continued and are supplemented by the introduction of stress management and relaxation techniques which further diminish the need for dysfunctional defenses.

The cognitive/behavioural interventions introduced from the previous stage are continued and are supplemented by the introduction of stress management and relaxation techniques which further diminish the need for dysfunctional defenses.

The group work interventions already in use are also continued. In addition role plays between the leaders and group members and the group members themselves are used to focus in a more useful way the rebellious behaviours. Supportive confrontation amongst the group members is encouraged. In fact, leader to member contact is more actively shifted to member to member contact. If the issues of this stage are not worked through then it is here that a high drop out rate can occur (Garland, Jones and Kolodny, 1973).

INTIMACY

It is at this phase that the formation of the group becomes evident. There is intensified interpersonal involvement among the group members, clarification of feelings. The group members feel more familial towards each other (Garland, Jones and Kolodny, 1973). The members begin to experience a sense of cohesiveness. This allows each group member to feel more comfortable with self-disclosure. Internally the rigid limitations of the traditional masculine ego idea begin to dissolve in favour of a self-concept that is more androgynous.

The men are able to give themselves permission to feel and express feelings and thus begin to internalize the values of the micro society which includes the social group work values. This is demonstrated through more observable communication directed from member to member. This indicates that the group members are beginning to assume leadership of their group which mirrors the ascribed group leadership. .

At this point the leaders' interventions become less apparent as they begin the process of transferring a large part of leadership to the group. At this juncture it is, therefore, extremely important to allow the group to begin setting sessional agendas.

DIFFERENTIATION PHASE

Reaching this phase indicates that the group has reached what has been referred to earlier as maturity (Lang, 1970, Sarri and Galinsky, 1974). This means that the group is an entity unto itself. The group members are setting their own agenda (Garland, Jones and Kolodny, 1973), usually through consensus; the individual needs are negotiated with the group-as-a-whole's needs. Trust and intimacy have been established. Now the most in-depth and critical work takes place in this environment. The group has become a micro society in which there is a resonance between the values, norms of the group and the ego ideal of the men in it.

Since it is only at this stage that major changes can be realized it is of crucial importance that a group meet for a minimum of 15 sessions in order to allow enough time to build up to this stage and then proceed through this stage to termination. Oftentimes this stage is short-circuited when in fact it needs to be maintained.

Formal group leadership is at a minimum and is reflected in the expectations of the group members that the group leaders function primarily as resource persons.

TERMINATION

This phase may be marked by denial, regression, need to continue, evaluation and flight (Garland, Jones and Kolodny, 1973). For this reason the worker's full leadership role becomes reactivated.

Termination needs to be introduced at least 4 to 5 sessions before it transpires.

The group leadership roles become reactivated, in normalizing, encouraging and modelling the various emotions associated with endings. It is also important for the group leaders to initiate group discussion around the question of informal continuation of member to member contact following the conclusion of the group. In our model an attempt is made to reduce the trauma around separation, to facilitate ongoing contact, and to support individual gains made by making available once monthly follow-up sessions for at least 3 months following termination.

CONCLUSION

In summary it is the vehicle of the mature group that contains and allows for the individual man to redefine the expectations he has of himself and to expand his effective and behavioural repertoire. This change flows from the integration of the values and norms which are at the heart of the group as a living entity and thus micro society. In this micro society each member is able to reconceptualize appropriate masculine behaviour based on a more androgynous view of humanity which reconciles the masculine and feminine in each individual. Thus this model operates multidimensionally to effect change, working simultaneously on the individual, the interactional and the societal levels. The process within the group mirrors the intrapsychic process in which defenses are reduced, restructured and rebuilt as the men move towards a more androgynous ego ideal. This model is, therefore, able to avoid a fragmentation and one dimensional approach of purely cognitive models.

REFERENCES

Beck, A. *Cognitive Therapy and The Emotional Disorders*. New York: New American Library, 1976.

Bern, E. and Bern, L. "A Group Program for Men Who Commit Violence Towards their Wives." *Social Work with Groups* (Spring 1984): 63-77.

Bernard, J.L. and Bernard, M.L. "The Abusive Male Seeking Treatment: Jekyll and Hyde." *Family Relations* (October 1984): 543-547.

Bograd, M. "Family Systems Approaches to Wife Battering: A Feminist Critique." *American Journal of Orthopsychiatry* (October 1984): 558-568.

Brisson, N. "Helping Men Who Batter Women." *Public Welfare* (Spring 1982): 29-34.

Burns, D. Feeling Good: The New Mood Therapy. New York: New American Library, 1980.

Cantoni, L. "Clinical Issues in Domestic Violence." *Social Casework* (January 1981): 3-12.

Christensen, C. and Pass, L. *A Social Interactional Approach to Counselling/ Psychotherapy.* Toronto: O.I.S.E. Press, 1983.

Coleman, K.H. "Conjugal Violence: What 33 Men Report." *Journal of Marital and Family Therapy* (April 1980): 207-213.

Currie, D. "A Toronto Model." *Social Work with Groups* (Summer 1984): 179-188.

Currie, D. "Group Model for Men Who Assault Their Partners." In *Understanding Wife Assault: A Training Manual for Counsellors and Advocates*, by Deborah Sinclair. Toronto: Ontario Ministry of Community and Social Services, 1985. Pp. 120-143.

Deschner, J. *The Hitting Habit: Anger Control for Battering Couples.* New York: The Free Press, 1984.

Deschner, J. et al. "A Treatment Model for Batterers." *Social Casework* (January, 1986): 55-60.

Dutton, D. "Wife Assaulters Explanations for Assault: The Neutralization of Self-Punishment." *Canadian Journal of Behavioural Science* 18 (4), 1986: 381-390.

Edleson, J. "Working with Men Who Batter." *Social Work* (May/June 1984): 237-242.

Ganley, A. *Court-Mandated Counselling for Men Who Batter: A Three Day Workshop For Mental Health Professionals.* Washington: Centre for Women Policy Studies, 1981.

Garland, J.A., Jones, H.E., and Kolodny, R.L. "A Model for Stages of Development in Social Work Groups." *Explorations in Group Work*, edited by S. Bernstein, Boston: Milford House, 1973. Pp. 17-71.

Glassman, U. and Kates, L. "Techniques of Social Group Work: A Framework for Practice." *Social Work with Groups* 9(1) (1986): 9-38.

Gold, J. A. "Incorporating Cognitive-Behavioural Techniques Into A Traditional Group Work Model." *Social Work with Groups* 4(3/4) (1981): 79-89.

Goldberg, H. *The Hazards of Being Male.* New York: New American Library, 1976.

Goldberg, H. *The New Male: From Macho to Sensitive But Still All Male.* New York: New American Library, 1979.

Gondolf, E. "Fighting for Control: A Clinical Assessment of Men Who Batter." *Social Casework* 65 (January 1985): 48-58.

Gondolf, E. *Men Who Batter: An Integrated Approach for Stopping Wife Abuse.* Holmes Beach, Florida: Learning Publications Inc., 1985.

Harris, S. and Sinclair, D. *Domestic Violence Project. A Comprehensive Model for Intervention.* Toronto Family Service Association, 1981.

Heppner, P. "Counselling Men In Groups." *The Personnel and Guidance Journal* (December 1981): 249-252.

Hoch, P. *White Hero and Black Beast: Racism, Sexism and the Mask of Masculinity.* London: Pluto Press, 1979.

Klein, A. *Social Work Through Group Process.* New York: SUNY Albany, 1970.

Lang, N. "Some Defining Characteristics of the Social Work Group: Unique Social Form." In *Social Work with Groups: Proceedings 1979 Symposium,* edited by Sonia Leib Abels and Paul Abels. Louisville, Kentucky: CASWG, 1981. Pp. 18-50.

Lewis, R. A. "Men's Liberation and the Men's Movement: Implications for Counsellors." *The Personnel and Guidance Journal* (December 1981): 256-259.

Neidig, P. and Friedman, D. *Spouse Abuse: A Treatment Program For Couples.* Champaign, Illinois: Research Press Co., 1984.

Northen, H. *Social Work with Groups.* New York: Columbia University Press, 1969.

Novaco, R. "Stress Inoculation Therapy for Anger Control." In *Innovations in Clinical Practice: A Sourcebook,* edited by P. Keller and L. Ritt. Sarasota, Florida: Professional Resource Exchange Inc., 1982. Pp. 181-200.

Papell, C.P., and Rothman, B. "Social Group Work Models: Possession and Heritage." In *Perspectives on Social Work Practice,* edited by A. Alissi. New York: The Free Press, 1980. Pp. 116-132.

Papell, C.P., and Rothman, B. "Relating the Mainstream Model of Social Work with Groups to Group Psychotherapy and the Structured Group Approach." *Social Work with Groups* 3(2).

Pressman, B. *Family Violence: And Treatment.* Guelph: Children's Aid Society, 1984.

Purdy, F. and Nickle, N. "Practice Principles for Working With Groups of Men Who Batter." *Social Work with Groups* (Fall/Winter 1981): 111-123.

Sarri, R. and Galinsky, M. "A Conceptual Framework for Group Development." In *Individual Change Through Small Groups,* edited by Glasser et al. New York: The Free Press, 1974. Pp. 71-89.

Saunders, D. "Helping Husbands Who Batter." *Social Casework* (June 1984): 347-356.

Sinclair, D. *Understanding Wife Assault: A Training Manual for Counsellors and Advocates.* Toronto: Ontario Ministry of Community and Social Services, 1985.

Star, B. et al. "Psychosocial Aspects of Wife Battering." *Social Casework.* (October 1979): 479-487.

Star, B. "Patterns In Family Violence." *Social Casework* (June 1980): 339-346.

Star, B. *Helping the Abuser: Intervening Effectively in Family Violence.* New York: Family Service Association of America, 1983.

Stein, T. "An Overview of Men's Groups." *Social Work with Groups* (Summer 1984): 149-175.

Taylor, J. "Structured Conjoint Therapy for Spouse Abuse Cases." *Social Casework* (January 1984): 11-18.

Tolson, A. *The Limits of Masculinity*. London: Tavistock Publications, 1977.

Vinter, R.D. "An Approach to Group Work Practice." In *Individual Change Through Small Groups*, edited by Glasser et al. New York: Free Press, 1974. Pp. 3-11.

Walker, L. *The Battered Woman*. New York: Harper, 1979.

Weidman, A. "Family Therapy With Violent Couples." *Social Casework* (April, 1986): 211-218.

Weitzman, J. and Dreen, K. "Wife Beating. A View of the Marital Dyad." *Social Casework* (May 1982): 259-265.

Wilson, G. and Ryland, G. "The Social Group Work Method." In *Perspectives on Social Group Work Practice*, edited by A. Alissi. New York: The Free Press, 1980. Pp. 169-194.

Yalom, I.D. *The Theory and Practice of Group Psychotherapy*. New York: Basic Books, 1975.

An Evaluation of a Group Program for Men Who Batter

Dennis Farley
Judith Magill

SUMMARY. This article describes a research study which evaluated a group service for men who batter. Change was evaluated both by self report and as interpreted from the Heimler Scale of Social Functioning. It was demonstrated that male batterers who entered into the group treatment process showed significant change with respect to human social functioning and in the cessation of physical violence towards their partners. Although the personal journey along which a batterer takes responsibility for his actions and finds appropriate coping mechanisms is intensely individual, this study adds to the literature which confirms that a supportive group experience can facilitate this process.

A group program for men who batter was developed in Montreal, Canada in 1983 in order to provide a therapeutic group milieu where participants could acknowledge their problem, assume responsibility for their actions and seek out appropriate alternatives to express actual and/or potential violence. This article describes a research study which evaluated this group service. Change was evaluated both by self report and as interpreted from the Heimler Scale of Social Functioning. It was demonstrated that male batterers who entered into the group treatment process showed significant change in social functioning and in the cessation of physical violence towards their partners. Although the personal journey along which a batterer takes responsibility for his actions and finds appro-

---

Dennis Farley, MSW, is Treatment Services Coordinator, Shawbridge Youth Centre, Montreal, Canada. Judith Magill is Associate Professor, McGill University School of Social Work, and is Co-Director of the McGill Family Violence Clinic, Montreal, Canada.

priate coping mechanisms is intensely individual, this study adds to the literature which confirms that a supportive group experience can facilitate the process.

LITERATURE REVIEW

Response to wife-battering has tended to fall into three areas: the provision of basic shelter for women, professional work with the couple, and work with the batterer. Offender treatment has become popular in North America in recent years; twenty-four programs now exist in Canada and an estimated two hundred in the United States (Browning, 1984). Most use a group approach and set cessation of the battering behavior as the major goal. The rationale for treating the batterer centers on the notion that he alone is responsible for the violence and on the knowledge that battering is most often a recurring behavior. Many women continue to live with their spouses despite repeated abuse. If separation does occur, the man may form another abusive relationship, thus perpetuating the cycle.

Although no stereotype clinical portrait exists of a man who batters, common characteristics have been identified particularly by Cantoni (1981) and Purdy and Nickle (1981). These include often intense isolation, role reversal and role confusion, inappropriate sexual expression, intense ambivalence and inconsistency, lack of trust, fear of dependence and independence, fear of intimacy, inability to play, inadequate ego structure, expectation of perfection, and lack of self-control. Abusive behavior is seen as the result of seeking explanations of internal turmoil through external sources. Batterers are not likely to seek help on the basis of a perceived problem of violence but rather on the basis of a precipitating factor such as the departure of the partner, or a court order.

Most existing services for batterers use groups as the therapeutic modality. The group format provides the opportunity for sharing of experiences and problems, mutual aid and the establishment of meaningful relationships outside the marriage (Toseland and Rivas, 1984; Ganley and Harris, 1978). Peer pressure is useful in dealing with denial and projection, both of which are common defense mechanisms of batterers. Most group programs share two basic assumptions: (1) Violence is a learned behavior and can be unlearned; (2) the man is solely responsible for his behavior and must accept this responsibility before the behavior can change. The cessation of violence is always the primary goal. The following objectives permeate treatment programs; having the batterer realize that he is not alone, that alternatives exist, that he can control himself and that battering is legally and morally unacceptable. In addition, some groups seek to increase awareness, confront social and emotional isolation and treat relationship problems. Other groups have the added objective of changing values and attitudes about men and women and establishing different norms for male-female relationships.

Treatment techniques vary among groups depending on goals and objectives. Behavior modification, skills training, relaxation training, cognitive restructuring and self-understanding are commonly used methods in helping men gain control and learn acceptable ways to manage anger (Edleson, 1984; Saunders, 1984). Insight producing techniques are used less frequently as the emphasis is on learning alternatives to violence in conflict resolution.

The use of groups to treat male batterers has gained widespread popularity in recent years. Initial results look promising and provide hope that batterers can be treated successfully. However, some critics fear that funding is being diverted from efforts to help the victims of abuse and is being prematurely allocated for offender treatment. The results of group treatment for batterers need evaluation before the modality is adopted on a wide scale basis as part of the program to treat wife abuse.

THE PROGRAM

Participants were recruited through the media and through information sessions with professionals who came into contact with wife abuse. Clients could self refer or be referred through a third party. However, the initial appointment had to be requested by the individual with the presenting problem in order to emphasize his assumption of responsibility. Funding was based on a fee for service model set on a sliding scale. Payment was individual and private.

All men who identified themselves as having been physically or psychologically abusive towards their partners were considered potential group participants. Although internal motivation for change was considered more desirable, candidates who identified their motivation as external, i.e., complying with a spouse's request, were also considered.

Group size was set at a minimum of three and a maximum of twelve. The group was open-ended in that members could enter or leave according to their schedules to avoid a waiting period as much as possible and to accommodate more members over time.

The group was directed by two male co-leaders who had experience in work with violence and with groups. Male co-leadership was seen as less threatening for clients who tend to project frustration toward their female partners. Co-leadership would increase the objectivity of intervention, provide mutual support for the group leaders and help facilitate interaction between group members.

The treatment process included twelve sessions of two and one half hours each. Sessions were held weekly and were audio recorded. The goal was to increase clients' awareness of issues and patterns. Two assessment interviews were structured to gather demographic information, case histories and client's perceptions of the presenting problem and to permit the administration of the Heimler Scale for Social Functioning (HSSF).

The initial demand for work stressed acceptance of responsibility for violent behavior, participation in forming a contract to attend meetings, payment for service, commitment to abide by basic group rules and identification of goals for change. The next stages focused on alternatives to violence, interpersonal skills development and personal awareness.

Two verbal contracts were made with each client. The group leader could require a written contract if necessary. In the first contract established at the individual interview, the client promised not to attend meetings under the influence of alcohol or drugs and promised not to attempt suicide during the period of attendance at group sessions. This latter commitment was assessed by a group leader through the first individual interview and through a client's response to two questions on the HSSF. A client unwilling to make these commitments could not participate in the group service. The second contract took place after two group meetings when the client committed himself to attend the remaining ten sessions. At the next-to-last session, the client could extend his commitment beyond twelve sessions if he could identify goals and the number of sessions he was willing to attend.

The clinical methodology was based on three premises: (1) Violence is an inappropriate learned coping mechanism of dealing with anger; (2) Men who batter are solely responsible for their violent behaviors; (3) The batterer must first increase awareness of his feelings in order to change.

A number of different therapeutic techniques were employed. The initial intervention created a "demand for work." Clients were encouraged to acknowledge responsibility for their violence and to make a commitment to stop. The use of a personal diary to heighten self-awareness was encouraged. Cognitive restructuring techniques helped make clients aware of self-defeating thoughts and assumptions and replace them with more positive and realistic ones. Interpersonal relationships and attitudes towards women were explored using the group process as a tool for change and growth.

Three months after the completion of the sessions, each client was requested to attend a one-hour individual follow-up interview with a group leader in order to gather information for evaluation and research. A follow-up questionnaire and the HSSF were administered.

METHODOLOGY

The research study was designed to evaluate whether the group program produced changes in social functioning and cessation of violence in men who batter. Data sources included clinical file notes, a pre-test and post-test of the HSSF, and a follow-up questionnaire.

The sample was composed of seventeen subjects who were the first to meet two control variables; attendance at twelve group meetings and attendance at a follow-up interview.

The HSSF assumes that the quantity and quality of frustration and satisfaction experienced by the individual at any given time determines his level of functioning in society. The format of the HSSF is the 1967 revised form; a French version identical to the English version was used with francophone subjects. The scale is made up of fifty-five questions divided into three sections: the Positive Index, the Negative Index, and the Synthesis.

Scoring

For the purpose of this study, the mean total scores for each index were used. Mean scores lower than 60 in the Positive Index suggest a need for therapeutic help. A score of 60 or above in this index is considered adequate, *providing* that the mean score on the Negative Index falls with 1/5 and 1/3 of the Positive mean score. The synthesis score should fall within an eight-point range of the Positive mean score. A Positive mean score of between 72 and 79, with the Negative mean score within 1/3 to 1/5 of the Positive mean score is considered normal functioning.

The HSSF was administered at points of intake and follow-up. A statistical analysis was carried out using "Repeated Measure Multi-Variate Analysis of Variance" to measure change in the Positive and Negative mean scores and Synthesis scores between the pre-test and post-test.

The follow-up questionnaire was administered orally by the group leader during the follow-up interview. It was designed to identify change as reported by the client; content included individual change, change in the partner, problems with physical and/or verbal violence and an evaluation of the group services received. Of the fourteen questions, nine concerned areas of change and five program evaluation.

For the purpose of this study certain questions were not included in the statistical analysis, and it was believed that their exclusion would not alter the results. The mean was calculated on the number of questions answered in the "desired" way and the number of questions responded to in the "least" desired manner. A "T" test with pooled variance was used in order to measure responses which significantly fell into the "desired" category. The number and percentage of clients who recidivated was calculated and specific areas of program evaluation were examined.

FINDINGS

Sample Characteristics

The sample size consisted of seventeen male subjects who completed the twelve group meeting commitment. The breakdown according to language included eleven in the francophone group and six in the anglophone which is the same for breakdown of mother tongue. The mean age of the subjects was 35.3 years, with a range in age from 23 to 52 years. Over 88% of the subjects worked full-time and approximately 82% (N = 14) were married or co-habiting and had at least one child. The majority of subjects appeared to be settled in work, to be involved in a relationship and to have begun a family.

At the point of intake, seven subjects were living with their partners. Of the ten subjects who lived apart, four reported their partners to be living in a shelter and six reported their partners to be living with family, friends or in separate accommodations. Of the seven subjects who lived together, four stated that a change of status was unlikely in the future while three subjects believed that separation was a possibility.

Clinical Observations

Clinical observations in this section refer to patterns and/or themes noted by the group leaders during individual and group sessions. Initially, most men presented in crisis. Generally, the partner had left or was threatening to do so. The men expressed fear of losing their partners and being unable to function on their own. Frequently, there was an antecedent of violence. The men often presented as feeling depressed, helpless and frustrated; in 30 to 40% of cases there was some mention of suicide. Very few were ready to assume responsibility for the violence; anger was directed at the spouse. The prime motivating factor for seeking help was the belief that group attendance would help bring back the partner.

. The men passed through similar patterns of addressing issues during the sessions. The spouse was initially perceived as the instigator of arguments. Through the middle sessions, this perception shifted more to focus on the individual. "Veteran" members were able to confront new members and diffuse many of the excuses made for behaviors. Feelings of depression often surfaced during this period. Many would begin to address underlying issues. A comradeship developed among members.

Towards and during termination sessions, depressed feeling subsided somewhat as members made tentative efforts to explore alternatives. They expressed hope and were more realistic in problem-solving. Many still presented as struggling but with a changed focus. Some appeared overly optimistic while others appeared overly concerned about the tasks ahead.

The Heimler Scale of Social Functioning

The HSSF examined the profile of social functioning before and after the group process as well as the significance of change over time (F $(3,14)$ = 5.1 P = .014). The mean Before Group scores (see Table 1) suggest that the average subject on entry is in some psychological/psychosocial crisis. This is concentrated in the Negative Index which implies an over-abundance of frustration in comparison to level of satisfaction. A need for support is strongly suggested. Although standard deviation scores show a large variance, even the most positive statistical composite (68% of the sample) still indicates the need for support.

TABLE 1

MEAN HSSF SCORES AND STANDARD DEVIATIONS

BEFORE AND AFTER GROUPS   (N = 17)

HSSF INDEX	BEFORE MEAN	GROUP STD DEV	AFTER MEAN	GROUP STD DEV	SIGNIFI-CANCE F	(1,16) P
POSITIVE	63.7	16.7	71.8	15.7	1.88	.189
NEGATIVE	43.8	13.4	23.1	16.7	16.10	.001
SYNTHESIS	58.6	17.2	73.4	12.3	6.61	.02

The After Group results show that the average subject falls within the range of a normal functioning person. The decrease of the Negative Index mean scores suggests that the average subject experi-

ences less frustration in his life at the point of follow-up. A proba-
ble decrease in feelings of depression and helplessness is also
implied suggesting that the subject found some alternatives to previously frustrating situations. Table 1 shows a very significant change
over time in the Negative and Synthesis mean scores (P = .001; P
= .02); the Positive mean scores were not quite significant. These
findings, along with an overall significance for the analysis of variance (p = level of social functioning from the point of intake to the
point of follow-up.

Follow-Up Questionnaire

As can be seen in Table 2, the mean score on the positive or most
desired response was significantly higher than the mean scores for
the least desired responses (T(30) = 4.00; P = .0005) suggesting
that on the average, subjects saw themselves as having changed and
felt that the group sessions were helpful. Questions addressing self-
change had 100% positive response. No subject had been physically
violent toward their partner since finishing the group sessions although 58% (n = 10) reported verbal abuse. Only eight subjects
felt they no longer had a problem with verbal abuse while fourteen
of the seventeen subjects felt they no longer had a problem with
physical violence.

The group was highly rated by the subjects; 100% would recom-

TABLE 2

MEANS AND STANDARD DEVIATIONS OF RESPONSES

ON FOLLOW-UP QUESTIONNAIRE (N = 16)

CATEGORY	MEAN	STD. DEV.
MOST DESIRED	11.37	4.06
LEAST DESIRED	5.62	4.06

mend the group to other men who batter, 86% believed it helped in terms of personal change, and the majority found the size and duration of the meeting appropriate. However, nine subjects felt that more meetings were needed. Eighty-eight percent of subjects felt that the group leaders understood them.

DISCUSSION

The goal of the group was achieved in that men who attended group meetings successfully ceased their battering behaviors and continued to be violence free at follow-up. This suggests that a major premise of program was confirmed; that men must acknowledge responsibility for their behavior prior to committing themselves to the cessation of physical violence as a means to cope with frustration in their relationships. Purdy and Nickle (1981) and Browning (1984) emphasize that responsibility, cessation of battering and the safety of the woman must be addressed before the issues underlying family violence can be treated.

The presenting problems of the subjects were consistent with what is suggested in the literature on group work practice. The results show that, at intake, most subjects were in crisis and did not tend to identify problems as existing within themselves. They demonstrated a lack of problem-solving abilities and carried a large amount of frustration. They expressed anger, usually toward the partner, and despair in those cases where the partner had left. These dynamics have been characterized in findings reported by Cantoni (1981), Ganley and Harris (1978) and Browning (1984). The "After-Group" results suggested that the subjects no longer appeared in crisis, and "After-Group" scores showed a level of social functioning which fell within the "normal" range (Heimler, 1975). It can be stated that the change over time is related to a sense of internal change since HSSF measures outcome from subjective reports. This is supported by the findings on the follow-up questionnaire where subjects identified the group as helping but pointed out that the change was a process they were responsible for. Thus both main objectives appear to have been achieved during the group process: these men stopped battering and also effected internal changes.

Strauss, Gelles and Steinmetz (1980), Cantoni (1981), Purdy and

Nickle (1981) and Browning (1984) emphasize that treatment for men who batter must focus on the individual and his violence and must provide support to him. The initial individual sessions provided immediate support. Men were more able to focus on their presenting problems because they attended without their partners. These individual meetings also eased some of the apprehension men experienced about sharing these problems with others.

Existing members facilitated entry into the group, and comradeship developed early on. "Veteran" members would confront angry and blaming statements and denial with reports of their own early experiences. These confrontations were well accepted as new members related to the "real" life examples of older members. The commonality identified by Shulman (1984) as the "all in the same boat" phenomena was evident.

The testing and conflict of the group's middle phases noted by Toseland and Rivas (1984) was also identifiable. Group leaders often had to engage in one-to-one dialogue within the group to provide support to members as they came closer to the underlying emotions associated with exposed conflicts and frustration. These one-to-one dialogues provided other members with information and a means to explore their own feelings. Anger diaries also proved helpful (Saunders, 1984).

Ending meetings were characterized by two distinctive responses. Some members felt that they had made significant inroads towards resolving problems and finding solutions while others were just beginning to address difficult and painful issues. This may explain why many subjects would have preferred more sessions. The range of "After-Group" scores suggests that some subjects were still struggling with issues. Results from the follow-up interview would correspond to Edleson's findings which noted a decrease in physical violence and an increase in expression of feelings and negotiations of conflict.

Limitations of the Research

Methodological limitations included small sample size and lack of control group. The follow-up questionnaire was not a tested tool and thus did not enhance the validity of the results. Its design did not lend to a range of statistical analysis and could only be analyzed in a simplistic fashion. Finally the nine-month time frame restricted this study. A longer follow-up period would have provided a better picture of the longevity of observed changes.

Implications for Future Practice

One finding from this research was the need expressed by the subjects to continue in a process of dialogue and support they felt from other group members. Although this particular group service was directed by its goal of the cessation of violent behavior, it appears clear that these men would benefit from an opportunity to continue to share and dialogue on issues which are of common concern. Such a need could be met through a self-help group of men who completed a treatment group, or through a second phase of group work provided by professionals working with family violence. Working with a couple after the man had completed a group process could also be explored in order to provide help in resolving problems in the relationship.

CONCLUSION

Despite methodological limitations, this research has demonstrated that entering a group process enables men who batter to significantly change with respect to social functioning and in the cessation of physical abuse. It provides an additional confirmation of the literature recognizing that treatment of the batterer is an important step in the global issue of family violence. The need for men who batter to address individually their violent behaviors is paramount because they alone are responsible for those behaviors and because sex-role stereotyping inhibits men from talking about their emotions. The provision of a focused, supportive group environment can assist men who batter along the personal journey through which they identify emotions and struggle to find appropriate coping mechanisms and provide a catalyst for individual change.

REFERENCES

Browning, J. *Stopping the Violence: Canadian Programmes for Assaultive Men.* National Clearinghouse on Family Violence, Health and Welfare Canada, 1984.

Cantoni, L. Clinical Issues in Domestic Violence. *Social Casework.* (January 1981): 3-12.

Edleson, J. Working With Men Who Batter. *Social Work.* (May-June 1984): 237-242.

Ganley, A. and Harris, L. Domestic Violence: Issues in Designing and Implementing Programs for Male Batterers. Presentation at American Psychological Association, 29 August, 1978.

Heimler, E. *Survival in Society.* London: Weidenfeld and Nicolson, 1975.

Heimler Foundation/Cardwell Human Resources Inc. *The Top Box Guide.* Saskatoon, 1984.

Purdy, F. and Nickle, N. Practice Principles for Working with Groups of Men who Batter. *Social Work with Groups* (Fall/Winter 1981): 111-123.

Saunders, D. Helping Husbands Who Batter. *Social Casework.* (June 1983): 347-353.

Shulman, L. *The Skills of Helping — Individuals and Groups.* 2nd. ed. Itasca: F.E. Peacock, 1984.

Strauss, M., Gelles, R., and Steinmetz, S. *Behind Closed Doors: Violence in the American Family.* New York: Anchor Press Doubleday, 1980.

Toseland, R. and Rivas, R. *An Introduction to Group Work Practice.* New York: Macmillan, 1984.

Group Therapy Techniques for Work with Child Sexual Abuse Victims

Elizabeth A. Sirles
Jane Walsma
Ruth Lytle-Barnaby
L. Claire Lander

SUMMARY. Group therapy techniques used by the Washington University Child Guidance Center's Child Sexual Abuse Treatment Team are described for clinicians working with child sexual abuse victims. Activities and tasks used to promote the therapeutic process are presented, broken down into three age groups: preschoolers, latency age children, and teenagers. The intent is to disseminate ideas found to be useful in the treatment process.

Child sexual abuse has been recognized as a social problem worthy of great attention and concern. As a result, numerous treatment programs have been developed to address this particular problem. Although there are model programs in existence that have received public acclaim, the vast majority of communities and social service agencies are struggling, trying to establish services that meet the needs of their clients, with the professional and fiscal resources available to them.

Program descriptions are becoming available to clinicians, pro-

Elizabeth A. Sirles, PhD, is affiliated with the University of Wisconsin-Milwaukee, School of Social Welfare, PO Box 413, Enders Hall, Milwaukee, WI 53201. Jane Walsma, MSW, Ruth Lytle-Barnaby, MSW, and L. Claire Lander, MSW, were affiliated with Washington University, George Warren Brown School of Social Work at the time of this writing. The junior authors may all be reached c/o L. Claire Lander, 1124 Ridgelynn Drive, St. Louis, MO 63124.

viding insight into the problem of child sexual abuse with a variety of suggestions for service delivery (Giarretto, 1982; Mayer, 1983; Sagroi, 1982). Such information is invaluable to providers and should be sought out by those interested in developing child sexual abuse treatment programs. General publications are also available, with less emphasis on treatment, covering a broader range of topics relevant to the problem (Meiselman, K.C., 1978; Mrazek and Kempe, 1981; Burgess, 1978). These frequently include case histories and summaries of the dynamics in the abusive household.

The literature addressing treatment of child sexual abuse tends to be programmatic, providing detail on the procedures involved in programs. Organizational structure, forms, case management issues and treatment modalities are carefully described. This clinical process information is useful but still leaves the clinician looking for content materials, or "how to" techniques that have been found to be useful in service delivery. The absence of such materials has been felt, with participants at national, regional, and local conferences on child sexual abuse demonstrating a thirst for knowledge of specific methods to be used when working with offenders, victims, and their families. Unfortunately, little information is available for filling the void.

The purpose of this paper is to provide clinicians with a summary of the techniques used by the Child Sexual Abuse Treatment Team at the Washington University Child Guidance Center. The intent is to disseminate ideas to practitioners who are working with victims of intrafamily child sexual abuse. The techniques described have been developed over the past four years, and draw from the expertise of the clinicians on the team. All of the techniques employed are used for the purpose of promoting an environment that is conducive to discussion of elements of the problem, peer support, and problem resolution. The techniques are means to the end of promoting the individual's healthy growth and development.

Techniques will be presented for working with children in three general categories: preschool (4-6), latency (7-11), and adolescent (12-17) age groups. Cutoff points are fairly arbitrary, with a child's maturity level being a better indicator of readiness for particular tasks.

PROGRAM DESCRIPTION

Since 1982, the Washington University Child Guidance Center in St. Louis, Missouri has concentrated approximately 30% of the clinical efforts toward working with intrafamily child sexual abuse cases. Over the course of time a variety of services have been developed, including: individual therapy for victims; parent and family therapy; and group therapy for victims, offenders, and nonoffending spouses. The treatment team has been composed of a child psychiatrist, psychologists, social workers, and social work graduate students, using a short-term, problem resolution therapeutic approach. Cases are referred by the state social service agency, juvenile courts, hospitals, prevention programs, and professionals in the community. Over two hundred and fifty victims have been referred for services, with the majority being girls (78%). The mean age is ten, with a range of 2 to 17 years old. Seventy-three percent are white, 26% black and 1% biracial.

Depending upon the circumstances of the case, either parent may be involved in therapy as an adjunct service to the child's treatment. The focus of this paper is on techniques used in the treatment of the children. Therefore, a full description of other services will not be provided. Most of the techniques described are used in victim's group therapy, but can be helpful when working with a child individually.

The Child Sexual Abuse Treatment Program (CSATP) has conducted a series of victims' groups, contingent upon the clientele's age and sex distribution. Groups for teenage and latency age girls have been ongoing for over three years. Additional groups, formed when size permits, have included: latency age group for boys, and groups for preschool age girls and boys. Group size ranges from three to ten members, with an ideal size of six children. Co-therapy teams are used to conduct groups, allowing for individual coverage if an emergency arises during group, or a leader is involved in nonclinical activities. Experience has taught that therapists working within a CSATP are frequently called upon to testify in civil, juvenile, or criminal court actions. These absences jeopardize the stability of regular group sessions if a co-therapist is not available.

Groups are conducted in 100 minute blocks on a weekly basis.

Clients are asked to make a commitment to a minimum of three months attendance, with continuance being optional. This structure allows for rotation through important content areas, and guarantees most clients the opportunity to participate in the discussions, regardless of when they enter the group process. This makes it possible to keep the groups open for admission at all times, thus preventing waiting lists and the accompanying problems. The immediate availability of services has been important for engaging clients in the group process, and providing crisis intervention.

PROGRAM GOALS

The CSATP has three general goals: guaranteeing protection from reabuse, promoting the physical health and emotional development of the child, and facilitating the development of a functional family system.

Although prevention of reabuse cannot be fully guaranteed, the team members take a position on child protection by playing a child advocacy role in the cooperation with other professionals involved with the case. This can include participation in the investigation, corroboration with protective service workers and court officials, and providing testimony in civil, juvenile, and criminal actions. The team invests nonclinical time to provide input into decision making that could affect the child's safety. In addition to child advocacy, prevention skills are taught to nonoffending spouses and children. This includes providing information about reporting, personal rights, and clarifying the abuser's sole ownership of responsibility for wrongful actions.

The physical health of the child is promoted by insuring appropriate medical care. When children enter the treatment program, an intake worker determines if the child has received proper medical attention. If not, a referral is made to a children's hospital Sexual Abuse Management Team that is qualified to provide a comprehensive examination, and full medical treatment. This can protect against the child suffering from unidentified physical manifestations of child sexual abuse (e.g., sexually transmitted diseases, pregnancy, damage to internal organs). And of equal importance, clarify for the child if there is any physical damage as the result of the abuse.

The child's emotional development is promoted by fully assessing behavioral and affective functioning in all the major social spheres, and providing treatment services accordingly. The child's self concept, and ability to function in the family, with peers, and in school are indicators of possible dysfunction that could arrest age-appropriate growth. Problems frequently encountered with these children's self concept include: feelings of responsibility for the abuse (being bad), poor body image (feeling ugly or dirty), and feelings of being damaged (broken, physically or sexually dysfunctional). Possible symptomatology that may be manifested as the result of these internalizations include: sleep or appetite disturbance, psychosomatic complaints, depressive symptoms, or signs of other behavioral or affective disorders.

Problems with peers can include: social isolation, aggressiveness, superficial relationships, and sexual acting out. School problems frequently involve declining grades, truancy, and poor achievement. An assessment of the functioning in all these social realms provides information for treatment planning.

Of key importance is an assessment of the child's functioning in the nuclear family. This includes an assessment of the entire family system to determine areas of dysfunction that may have contributed to the abuse occurring. Briefly, the mother/child, father/child, and mother/father subsystems are assessed. Dyadic work ensues to develop an open, protective alliance between the nonoffending parent and child, including strategies for protection and a plan for reporting subsequent abuse. Dyadic work with the abuser and child is only arranged when the abuser admits to the abuse, accepts full responsibility for his actions and is able to apologize to the child. Dyadic work with these individuals is geared toward learning appropriate styles of communicating and relating, work toward forgiveness, and the achievement of a mutually beneficial relationship. The parental/marital subsystem receives treatment with the goal of promoting open communication, appropriate means of relating as a spouse and parental unit, and a plan for the protection of the child(ren). Upon completion of these tasks, the family is brought together in family therapy to work toward reunification and healthy functioning.

Combined, these efforts provide a comprehensive treatment program, sensitive to the needs of the child in a dysfunctional family.

PRESCHOOL AGE CHILDREN

Working with preschool age children (4-6-year olds) is both the most difficult and most rewarding work in the program. A great deal of patience and creativity is involved in the process of helping young children resolve the conflicts and fears in their lives. Presenting problems include: separation problems, unusual fearfulness, sexually explicit behavior, regression to infant-like behaviors, and sleep disturbance with nightmares or night terrors. In addition to working with the parents, "play therapy" is useful for helping resolve the problems. Individual therapy is the mode of choice initially to establish a relationship with the therapist (group leader) and begin group preparation. Parallel play (playing alongside of the child, loosely imitating activities) and playing nonthreatening, noncompetitive games are helpful for establishing contact and building a rapport. Preferably, therapy can be conducted in the group room to establish a sense of comfort and familiarity with the environment. The use of coloring books (Preschool, 1984) and books (Boegehold, 1985; Williams, 1980) on prevention of sexual abuse are helpful for introducing concepts and engaging children. As materials are expensive, copying key pages to color can be helpful.

The therapy room should be equipped with child sized furniture, drawing materials, noncompetitive games (e.g., blocks, play money), puppets (including all family members), play telephones, a play house, and anatomically correct dolls (including all family members, in black and white races). Each toy can be used as a tool in promoting self-expression and working toward problem resolution.

Once children are comfortable in the setting, appear to feel safe with the therapist, and are free of excessively disruptive behaviors, they are moved into group therapy. The use of peers for support, information sharing, and activity stimulation is felt to be superior to individual therapy. The children benefit from the friendships developed and are more verbal in this setting. However, children who are not adequately prepared or "group ready," may be too agitated or withdrawn to benefit from peer contacts. In either group or individual therapy, the following ideas have been useful in working with preschool age children.

Sessions begin with sitting quietly on the floor and reviewing room rules. Children benefit from an awareness of expectations, and a sense of control in the environment. Rules include: no interrupting, hitting, or rough play. Time out chairs are in the room, being available for providing a place to calm down while still in the session. Frequently, a therapist will stay with a child during time out to provide reassurance. When a child becomes distressed, this is a means for helping to reduce tension.

Several techniques are employed to aid in the discussion of sexual abuse. Fantasy play is used to promote feelings of safety and open communication. The children "fly" with the therapists around the room, landing on their "magic carpets" (mats) in a "magic place" called Shazmoo, "where you are allowed to talk about secrets and anything that is important to you." Children enjoy the game and attach a sense of specialness to these discussions because of the way they are framed. Content areas discussed include: appropriate touching, reporting abuse, feelings about the abusive and nonabusive parents/relatives, human sexuality, sex play with self and peers, the adult's responsibility for the abuse, and testifying in court. Children are encouraged to talk to each other about their feelings and experiences, using any of the tools present in the room as aids. After "flying back" to the center, a puppet show or role play exercise may be used to let the children act out elements of the discussion held in Shazmoo. This allows for therapists to assess the children's understanding of the material discussed, and ability to act on the knowledge. Feedback and further discussion can ensue.

A break is taken midsession, with nonsugar snacks and use of the bathroom. Social relationships are encouraged in discussion and a free play period. The final segment of the group involves teaching relaxation exercises and guided imagery to "fun" or "happy" places. Skills already learned can be helpful during stressful moments in the group and are positively reinforced when exhibited.

In total, these activities provide for a variety of means to communicate with children and help them learn appropriate personal and social skills. Each activity lasts approximately fifteen minutes, allowing time for transitions between tasks and the break. Group success is dependent upon the leaders' skill and ability to relate to children in this age group, and the children's group readiness.

LATENCY AGE CHILDREN

While the preschool age therapy groups are mixed with boys and girls, children between seven and eleven are separated into boys' and girls' therapy groups. Due to the sensitive nature of the material discussed, these children need to be free to relate comfortably with their same sex peers.

Although play continues to be an important means of self-expression, children in this age group are more capable of discussing their feelings and problems. Therefore, more direct group discussions can spontaneously emerge. A variety of mediums are used to stimulate these discussions, with topic areas selected. A single exercise is planned for each week, designed as a catalyst to open communication in the group. Drawings, puppet shows, role playing, and letter writing have been effective tools for this purpose.

A five-part sequential drawing exercise is used to help children examine the abuse process over time. Each week in a five week series, the children are asked to draw a picture showing one of the following: (1) "What it was like before the abuse"; (2) "What it was like the first time it happened"; (3) "What it was like during the time you were being abused"; (4) "What it was like when you told someone"; and (5) "What you think your future will be like." Instructions are deliberately vague, leaving the option for various interpretations. Children may draw pictures depicting themselves, their families, or particular events they recall from that particular time period. Group discussions can then be focused on these different perspectives of the event. As time permits, children are asked to put on puppet shows, acting out the scene in their drawings. They use their peers to act in the show, instructing them on their role.

Each phase in the drawing sequence provides information about the children's perceptions of themselves, and the abuse. The final drawing in the sequence provides an opportunity to assess the children's sense of hope or resolution. This process provides content for the therapeutic process, moving children through the abusive period in their lives, while focusing on key events.

Subsequent to the drawing series, several weeks are spent with letter writing exercises. Two letters each are written to: the abuser, nonabusive parent(s), and other important parties (i.e., judges, social service workers, foster parents). Each week is spent writing to one individual. First, a letter that will not be delivered is written. Children are encouraged to write anything they feel or have wanted to say. Group discussion follows, sharing letters between members, focusing on content that the writer feels is too sensitive to actually reveal to the individual. A second letter is then written that would be delivered to the individual. Letters written to abusive or nonabusive parents are delivered during the adult group therapy sessions. The adults also write similar letters, to provide for the opening of communication through a safe medium. Letters are not censured or screened for negative material, as the group provides for peer support when painful exchanges occur. The contents of letters reflect the interactive patterns between the family members, as well as attitudes and beliefs about the abuse.

Children and parents are frequently distressed by the social service and judicial systems they are involved with. Writing letters to key individuals, to send or destroy, provides an outlet for ventilating concerns or frustration. Children are not pressured to send letters they feel are volatile, as they are frequently good judges of the consequences for their actions. Confrontation can occur during dyadic therapy at a later date.

In the final phase of the group program, several weeks are spent on sex education. Sexually abused children have a great deal of misinformation about sexuality, their bodies, and reproduction. Anatomically correct dolls and age appropriate sex education publications (Mayle, 1973, 1975, 1977; Aho and Petras, 1978; Gordon, 1973, 1974) are used to help clarify their level of knowledge, and to provide them with correct information. Discussion needs to include material on age appropriate sexual activities, and relationships with opposite sex peers. Material should be reviewed for several weeks, using nontechnical terminology. Children frequently discuss the abuse during this phase, questioning their physical health and the long-term consequences of the abuse. These discussions are important for the healing process, as they correct misunderstandings and empower children with knowledge.

As with the preschoolers, the latency age group takes a break from activities approximately midway through the session for a snack and free play. Phone numbers are exchanged and friendships emerge. Follow-up has revealed that some of these friendships have become mutually beneficial, long-term relationships.

TEENAGERS

Working with teenage victims is qualitatively different than working with younger children because of the developmental tasks facing teenagers and their level of verbal skills. Teenagers are capable of "talk" therapy and can function with less structure in their therapy sessions. However, they express a preference for activities, and participate more actively in task-oriented therapy.

Developmentally, teenagers are working toward individuation from their parents, forming primary attachments to their peers. Teenagers are developing their psychosexual identities and moving toward opposite sex partnering.

Sexual abuse occurring during this stage can be detrimental to the completion of these tasks and retard the normal course of psychosocial/sexual development. Individuation cannot evolve when major problems between the parent(s) and teenager exist. Teenagers frequently leave problem families in revolution, failing to resolve the conflicts and disrupting their ability to relate to their families.

Therapy for teenage victims needs to assist in confrontation of the problem, and provide a careful examination of the psychological effects of the abuse. Flashbacks, sexual promiscuity or aversion, may be the result of an abusive sexual relationship. Therefore, therapy needs to be a forum for discussing these issues and providing information useful to building a healthy sense of the sexual self.

All teenage victims in the CSATP are given a copy of Ruth Bell's book *Changing Bodies, Changing Lives*. This has served as a valuable resource because it was written for teenagers, covering a wide range of topics relevant to their specific needs. Group discussions can be stimulated from material presented on: forced sex, female and male anatomy, sexual relations, birth control, friendships and family problems. These discussions can be enhanced by using excerpts and illustrations from the book. Each topic can be related to the abuse and the teenagers' current perceptions of their lives.

In addition to the book, techniques are used in therapy to generate discussion. When discussing family problems, sculpting the family using peers as figures in the family is useful for exemplifying feelings and dynamics that contribute to the family's dysfunction. Charting genograms while exploring feelings about members of the family can also promote discussion that may be difficult otherwise. The letter writing exercises previously described are used to aid in self-expression, and relaxation exercises are taught as methods of anxiety reduction.

A popular exercise in the teenage group is the joint production of a videotaped film. The topic can vary by group decision, but has to be related to child sexual abuse. Ideas have included: how it feels to be a victim, how to identify an abuse victim, how to report abuse, confronting the offender, testifying in court, and "saying NO." Group members enjoy the task and benefit from the support the exercise can generate. Films are only viewed by the group unless members unanimously agree to have a particular film shown to the adult groups.

Combined, these activities or tasks provide teenagers with some structure to assist them in bringing out important material that needs to be talked about. Despite their age and verbal skills, they have difficulty discussing sensitive issues and benefit from the aids presented.

CONCLUSION

Work with child sexual abuse victims can be enhanced by the use of activities, tasks, and techniques for generating discussion. This paper has described methods used by the Washington University Child Guidance Center's Child Sexual Abuse Treatment Team. Ideas presented demonstrate the value of creativity in program development, illuminating a myriad of ways clinicians can stimulate children to examine their lives and themselves.

REFERENCES

Aho, J. and Petras, J. (1978) *Learning About Sex: A Guide for Children and Their Parents*. New York: Holt, Rinehart, and Winston.

Bell, R. (1980) *Changing Bodies, Changing Lives*. New York: Random House.

Boegehold, B. (1985) *You Can Say "NO"*. Racine, WI: Western Publishing Co.

Burgess, A. et al. (1978) *Sexual Assault of Children and Adolescents*. Lexington, MA: Lexington Books.

Giarretto, H. (1982) *Integrated Treatment of Child Sexual Abuse*. Palo Alto, CA: Science and Behavior Books, Inc.

Gordon, S. (1973) *Facts About Sex for Today's Youth*. New York: The John Day Co.

Gordon, S. (1974) *Girls are Girls and Boys are Boys: So What's the Difference?* New York: The John Day Co.

Mayer, A. (1983) *Incest: A Treatment Manual for Therapy with Victims, Spouses, and Offenders*. Holmes Beach, FL: Learning Publications.

Mayle, P. (1973) *Where Did I Come From?* NJ: Lyle Stuart, Inc.

Mayle, P. (1975) *What's Happening to Me?* NJ: Lyle Stuart, Inc.

Mayle, P. (1977) *Will I Like It?* New York: Corwin Books.

Meiselman, K.C. (1978) *Incest: A Psychological Study of Causes and Effects with Treatment Recommendations*. San Francisco, CA: Jossey-Bass, Inc.

Mrazek, P. and Kempe, H., eds. (1981) *Sexually Abused Children and Their Families*. Elmsford, NY: Pergamon Press.

Preschool Press. *It's OK to Say No Coloring book*. New York: Playmore, Inc.

Sgroi, S.M., ed. (1982) *Handbook of Clinical Intervention in Child Sexual Abuse*. Lexington, MA: Lexington Books.

Williams, J. (1980) *Red Flag, Green Flag People*. Fargo, ND: Rape and Abuse Crisis Center, PO Box 1655, Fargo, ND 58107.

Use of Group Work to Help Children Cope with the Violent Death of a Classmate

Judy Haran

An ever-increasing number of school-age children are experiencing the loss of a classmate as a consequence of homicide, or other violent means of death. According to recent crime statistics, 4.9% of murder victims are under 14 years of age. Their deaths result from firearms, physical child abuse, asphyxiation, and other forms of fierce maltreatment. The perpetrators are usually family members, or persons known to the family (Uniform Crime Reports, 1985).

The impact of a catastrophic event, such as the loss of a friend due to violent death, may have far-reaching repercussions. While the emotional and psychological impact of loss and death on children has frequently been addressed in the literature, it is usually directed at helping children to cope with the natural or accidental death of a parent, sibling, or teacher (Brooks, Silverman et al., 1985; Prichard and Collard, 1977). There is sparse information, however, which speaks to the issue of coping with loss by homicide, and that body of literature addresses itself to the needs of family members surviving homicide victims (Getzel and Masters, 1984). This paper will examine the effect of the sudden, violent death of a child on his classmates, and will utilize the broad framework of the Mainstream Model of Social Work with Groups to describe how the group work approach can be used to create a natural helping network that provides coping skills, mutual aid, and support. The Mainstream Model of Social Work with Groups, devel-

Judy Haran is Clinical Assistant Professor, University of Maryland, School of Social Work and Community Planning, 525 West Redwood Street, Baltimore, MD 21201.

oped by Papell and Rothman (1980), encompasses a systemic construct that allows intervention at the interface of the individual in the classroom, the classroom as a whole, and the school environment. In addition, this flexible model enables the worker to incorporate multiple leadership roles which are related to the identified tasks and needs of the group.

THE CHILD'S CONCEPT OF DEATH

To provide effective intervention in time of crisis, the worker must be knowledgeable in child development, since coping is influenced by the child's perception of death and the meanings attributed to it at different maturational stages. As early as the 1940s, studies emerged which established the framework for viewing the death concept as a developmental phenomenon (Anthony, 1940; Nagy, 1948). Further evidence has emerged since the 1960s supporting a developmental focus for understanding death concepts from both predominantly Piagetian and psychoanalytic perspectives (Miller, 1971). Recent research also indicates that the development of the death concept is related to both chronological age and the development of receptive language skills, general knowledge, and verbal concept formation.

The preschool child thinks about the world from the limited perspective of his own experience. The preschooler's thought process is classified by Piaget as preoperational and characterized in all aspects by his egocentrism. This is illustrated by magical thinking, for example, when the young child feels responsible for his thoughts and wishes being enacted in the world. Thus, an external event may be interpreted by the child as a direct result of his fantasies or statements.

Preschool children have extremely variable ranges in their ideas of what constitutes living, and of what cessation of living, or death entails. The preschool child will respond to encounters with death based on his own experiences, his family's religious and cultural beliefs, his own attachment with the dead person, and his developmental level. A child attending the funeral of his grandmother may leave a group of grieving relatives to run out happily to play with friends. His grief is not resolved, but his attention span is short. His grief will be manifest through recurrent play patterns, repetitive questions, and insistence that grandmother will return "when she is finished dying." Another child may respond to the death of a pet with ritualistic burial ceremonies, which may include digging up and reburying the body in an attempt to master and understand the vague concept of finality and permanence. A preschool child may respond to sibling death with many emotions that range from sadness to elation to guilt. Egocentrism and magical thinking may lead her to think that her wishes and normal sibling rivalry caused the death to occur.

The child's responses to death and loss must be viewed in the family context. The response of the family system at the time of the death, and in the early crisis period, will strongly influence the response of the child. The family response may well govern whether or not the child achieves adaptation to, and resolution of, the loss. Raphael (1983) identifies several family variables which influence the child's reaction:

1. The family in which death is a taboo: Death and loss are never discussed in some families. Conspiracies of silence reign. The child senses frightening secrets, but knows it is taboo to ask about them.
2. The family in which someone must be to blame: The family pattern has long been one of finding fault; when death occurs, the search for a cause and a person to blame predominates, and guilt is the main emotion that clouds the response to the death. The child in this family learns that death is caused by someone, and that anger and guilt, not mourning, is the natural response.
3. The family in which things must go on as before: In some families loss and change must be denied or delayed. The system is one that has refused to acknowledge other changes long before this death has occurred. The child gets the message that he must not grieve and that the role lost through death will be filled by someone else.
4. The family that functions with openness and sharing of feelings: In this family, relationships are valued, feelings are expressed, and patterns are established for coping with positive

and negative experiences. The child learns that loss can be mastered, and that the care and consolation offered by others can be healing. (pp. 114-117)

Bowlby (1980) outlines a number of factors which he believes to be associated with the more favorable outcome of childhood bereavement. The influencing variables include:

1. the causes and circumstances of the death, including what the child is told and what opportunities are given to him subsequently to enquire about what happened;
2. the family relationships after the loss;
3. the patterns of relationship within the family prior to the loss.

The preschooler's responses to loss may be exaggerated when the death has occurred through homicide or other violent means. Seeking to protect the preschooler, family members may not tell him about the incident, or may create a less traumatic explanation. However, children may hear or perceive different versions regarding the means of death, and may rely on their imaginations, creating a much more fearful situation than may have actually occurred. Other adults may become overprotective of the child, and may unknowingly reinforce the child's fears that the same fate may befall him. The child's normal coping mechanism of mastery through repetitive questions may not be tolerated by adults who want to avoid discussion of the tragedy. Thus the preschool child may become quite anxious, and may manifest behaviors of separation anxiety, bedwetting, and eating or sleeping disturbances.

The period of childhood from 6 to 10 years is described as latency by Freud and industry by Erikson. Piaget classifies the cognitive processes as concrete operational. The child begins to view the world from an external point of view, and language becomes communicative and less egocentric. Parents become less omnipotent, as the child enters the school world where the teacher and other adults become the models for identification. During this period, the child develops the capacity for feelings of guilt. The identification with parents in the oedipal resolution, as well as by a variety of other processes becomes the basis for the superego, and the child's capacity to feel guilt for events that have happened or might happen. Magical thinking persists, but the child is better able to test reality.

The child's concept of death also evolves rapidly, and is dependent on the influences of the family, religion, socioeconomic status, and the child's own life experiences, as well as his cognitive abilities. In a 1948 study, Nagy found that two-thirds of the children between the ages of 5 and 9 personified death either as a separate person, or as identified with the dead person. Other research cites children as believing death has a moral connotation — that death is punishment for wrongdoing (McIntire and Angle, 1972). During this age, children understand that death is not reversible and that it can happen to anyone, including themselves.

During the latency period, children apply their developing cognitive skills to mastering the concept of death. They may show an interest in funerals or cremation, even requesting to go to the funeral of a relative. There may be much curiosity about the effect of the cessation of life on a human body. Children who have lost a pet may have an elaborate funeral only to dig up the body several days later to examine the remains. This may occur for several days without any sign of distress in the child, until he has learned enough from the situation. The child's reaction to the death of an adult or young person may range from sadness to anger to fear or anxiety. He may attempt to handle his feelings by discussing the situation with friends or adults, but he may not know appropriate behavior and may be fearful of crying or expressing other emotion. It is not unusual for the child to become anxious, or develop various physical complaints, such as headache or stomachache, and fear that he may be dying too. Because the child is more acutely aware of death as a personal possibility for himself, he may become frightened of sleep and darkness, by equating them with times of death.

As with younger children, adults may seek to protect latency age children from details of child homicide, or other violent means of death. These children, however, are equally likely to discover the tragedy from an account on the radio, television, or newspaper, and may know of the event before their parents find out. The child in this age range is usually shocked by news of the death. He may show considerable denial, or sometimes, great anxiety and distress. Some children in this group will try to carry on as if the death means nothing to them, going on with their play, or acting in some cheerful, yet obviously brittle, manner. This is usually transient, and the child's tearful distress soon breaks through (Raphael, 1983). School administrators and teachers may feel uncomfortable discussing the deceased child with students, and may cope with their emotions by proceeding with scheduled lesson plans. Parent-child conflict may arise regarding details of the child's death, attendance at the funeral or cemetery, or even appropriate expressions of sympathy. Parents may feel unable to provide their child with an adequate explanation for such an illogical event. Conflict may also arise in school as teachers grapple with what to tell students, and what, if any, type of activity or memorial program should be planned for the deceased child.

The developmental changes during adolescence make death seem impossible. The early part of adolescence is marked by real concern with body image, and turmoil resulting from tremendous swings in mood and behavior. The adolescent experiences changes in body growth and shape, as well as the appearance of secondary sexual characteristics. Teenagers become increasingly distant from parents and demonstrate intense interest in the peer group and extrafamilial young adults who tend to become superheroes. The denial of his mortality is manifested by the adolescent's death-denying involvement with speeding vehicles and experimentation with drugs and alcohol. The adolescent's goal of identity is accomplished through mastery of the developmental tasks of achieving a stable self-concept, independence from family, an adult sexual role, and the selection of a vocation (Erikson, 1968).

By age 12, the child generally has an understanding of the elements necessary for a mature concept of death: universality, inevitability, irrevocability, finality, cessation of bodily functions, natural etiology, and permanence. His ability for abstract thought enables him to think about his own death. Denial is utilized to cope with the anxiety elicited by these thoughts of his mortality. The death of a peer, for him, is a cataclysmic reaffirmation of his own mortality.

The adolescent who is dealing with the violent death of a classmate may have a variety of reactions. Utilizing denial, he may find a number of reasons why the same thing could not happen to him.

He may project his anxieties onto his classmates, and attempt to console others as a means of comforting himself. Depending on the degree of identification which the adolescent has with the dead child, as well as his own ego strengths, he may relate to the healthier, more mature members of the class, or become depressed, and isolated in his grief. It is not uncommon for adolescents to imitate and identify with persons in their environment. It is particularly crucial when this identification is with one who has died. If carried to an extreme, this process can lead to suicidal attempts or suicide. Most adolescents have a greater capacity to deal with death than does the younger child. They are more able to cope with the immediate impact of the tragedy, to mourn, and to resume and continue their emotional life in harmony with their level of maturity. They are more likely to take an active role in funerals, and participate in memorials to the dead.

CONCEPTUAL MODEL FOR INTERVENTION

The Mainstream Model of Social Work with Groups provides a framework which supports a social systems approach to crisis intervention in the classroom, and permits the incorporation of theories of human behavior. Recognizing the dynamic interaction of the individual child, his family, the classroom, and the school environment, this model conceptualizes reality as systems of related entities and identifies multiple levels of intervention. The mutual goal is to help each level recognize its adaptive capacity to respond to the tragedy, and provide opportunity for mastery and growth.

There are several avenues from which the social worker can offer crisis intervention to help students cope with the violent death of a classmate. If part of the school system, the worker may be asked by administrators or teachers to function as a resource person for classroom children, or to provide individual counseling to a child. Alternatively, a social worker from outside of the school system may be approached by concerned parents, and asked to assist a group of children share their concerns and reactions. As an outsider, the worker must recognize the natural boundaries that exist in the school, and must first gain sanction from the principal to enter and work within the system. Once entry has been accessed, collaborative planning with school administrators can result in an integration of the worker's goals, and the goals of the children, the classroom group, the parents, and the school, a process of common goal development which is one of the fundamental concepts of the Mainstream Model of Social Work with Groups.

Another salient point of the model is its conception of the group as a mutual aid system. The group is viewed as "an alliance of individuals who need each other, to varying degrees, to work on certain common problems. The important fact is that they need each other, as well as the worker" (Schwartz, 1961). The group has within it the power to develop a system that will both help each member to help himself and others, and that will, "through the collective power and action of the group . . . influence, modify, or contribute to its environment" (Papell and Rothman, 1980). The classroom is viewed as a naturally formed group which has the inherent capacity for problem-solving, decision-making, and mutual support. It needs only the facilitation of the worker to mediate the process, encourage the sharing of data, and foster the work of the group.

The concept of indigenous leadership is another facet of the Mainstream Model of Social Work with Groups. The worker may take a variety of roles within the group, such as teacher or facilitator, but also views the classroom teacher, and perhaps other students, as sharing internal leadership responsibilities. Encouragement of group member's assumption of leadership tasks and functions ensures the continuity of problem-solving and support above and beyond the formal group session into the normal classroom week.

According to Papell and Rothman (1980), activities in the mainstream group are spontaneously generated by members and are implemented by the group in a planful process. Thus, the needs of the group turn into tasks directed at achieving the group's overall purpose. Each member provides an important contribution to the group in terms of his understanding of the task, and the unique perspective he brings into the group. The worker who provides intervention at the interface of the child, class, family, and school can help each level to develop meaningful activities designed to promote understanding of the tragedy and facilitate the grief process.

APPLICATION OF THEORY TO PRACTICE

The application of the above principles to group work practice will be discussed in the example of a single session group which was used to provide intervention following the murder of a nine-year-old boy by his father, who subsequently committed suicide. The child was immediately cremated, and there was no funeral or memorial service. The tragedy occurred during winter vacation, and parents of classmates questioned whether to tell the children, how to do this, the impact it would have on them, and how they could help the children cope. The school questioned the role it should play in the process, if any. The worker, called in as a consultant by the parents, spoke first with the parents to assess their concerns and needs, and then jointly with the parents developed a tentative plan to present to school administrators. It was felt that a group session in which children could discuss the child's death and their feelings and fears about it would be the best approach to take. The proposal included a voluntary evening group session for children and parents, co-led with the worker and classroom teacher. Although reluctant to become involved, the principal agreed to sanction the meeting and support the classroom teacher's involvement, provided the session was not held in the school. Thus, the pre-group communications opened access into the class, helping the administrators to understand how children might react to the sudden death of a friend, and to formulate their own role in supporting the children's work. The worker agreed to be available as a resource to any additional staff or students who had concerns regarding the child's death. It became clear from the preliminary discussions with the parents that there was an equal need for the parents, as well as the children, to meet as a group to discuss the death and their own reactions to it. The worker decided to ask another worker to lead a parallel parent group which would meet at the same time as the children's group. One parent made arrangements to meet in a local church, and another called all of the parents in the class.

It was planned that the group sessions would meet for two hours. Recognizing that even a single session group goes through distinct stages of beginning, middle, and end, the worker organized the activity within specific time frames. The first half-hour of the group was a warm-up period which included parents and children; the worker had not previously met the children, the classroom teacher, nor most of the parents. Introductions were made, and a "contract" for the evening was discussed. The purpose of the warm-up time was to allow parents and children to develop a sense of trust in the worker, to allow the children to regain a preexisting feeling of group cohesion, and to allow a period of time for anxiety about the group and the topic to diminish before the work began in earnest. During this time, the worker asked the children, parents, and teacher to tell her about the child, since she had never met him; the group responded by sharing memories about his friendship, his sense of humor, and his activities in class. This was followed by a discussion of how class would be different when the children returned from vacation.

The children and parents then separated into two groups, with the worker and teacher remaining with the children. The goals of both groups were to exchange information about the deaths of the father and son, to discuss the grief process, to share mutual feelings, and to develop a plan for a memorial program. Following the individual groups, the children and parents regrouped and met briefly at the end with the worker for refreshments.

The worker began the children's group by asking if anyone had ever lost a friend or relative through death. The children compared experiences they had had with illness, funerals and mourning. The worker then asked the children what they thought was different about this occasion, which opened a taboo area—the fact that this was a friend who was murdered by his father. Noticing that the children were moving restlessly, and avoiding eye contact, the worker changed the focus slightly, and suggested an activity: Slips of paper and pencils were passed around, and children could anonymously write down any question they would like to ask about the child's death. This helped to release tension and anxiety; before answering the questions, the worker asked if anyone had been told what had happened to the child. Not all of the children knew, and each shared what they had been told by their parents, or had seen on television. Their teacher asked how hearing this made them feel, and the children talked of being angry at the boy's father, and sad at the loss of their friend. Wondering about guilt, the worker asked if anyone was worried that they should have done something earlier. Several children were concerned that they had noticed the father's moods and were sorry they hadn't told their parents. This opened the discussion of why a father would do this to his son, preceding another taboo area: the children's conscious fears that something like this could happen to someone else, or even themselves. Several children felt this could happen "if you made your dad angry, or didn't listen," and one fragile child became very anxious during the discussion. Others, using denial and bravado to master uncomfortable feelings, demonstrated how they could physically overcome anyone who tried to harm them. After a brief respite for tension release, the teacher then asked them to think of all the reasons why it probably wouldn't ever happen. He then proceeded to read the questions they had written. Their questions very much reflected their developmental level, and their intellectual attempt to master all the implications of what had happened, and to some extent, the meaning of death: How exactly did he die? Is he in Heaven or Hell? What happens to ashes after cremation? What can we do in memory of him? The leaders encouraged the group members to answer as many of the questions as they could, using a problem-solving approach. To teach the children about typical reactions to death and grief, the worker asked if anyone was experiencing dreams or nightmares, or was fearful of going to bed. Some children had these concerns, and others were uncomfortable leaving their parents for any period of time. The leaders assured the children that these feelings were normal, and helped the children identify classmates, or other adults that they could talk with if they so desired.

The leaders reflected that someone had asked what they could do in memory of the child. The children had various ideas, and the worker suggested that several children and parents as well as the teacher could form a committee which would be responsible for planning a memorial project that represented their memories of their friend.

The parallel meeting for the parents addressed many of the same issues as the children's meeting. They began by sharing common concerns regarding their children's reactions, their own reactions, and their loss of confidence in their own judgement, as well as their guilt, since some knew the child's father fairly well. Other parents worried that their children were fearful that the same fate could befall them, and one father, who was quite depressed, worried that he might do the same thing to his child. The parents focused on the theme of "what could cause a father to do that to his child," as if, like their children, they were attempting to gain mastery through intellectual understanding and by distancing the situation from themselves.

The parents then focused on their children's reactions, noting that some were more timid, and some more affectionate, towards their fathers. The group discussed what this might mean, and the worker suggested that they reassure their children that it was not the fault of the child that the tragedy occurred, and that no child could cause an adult to do such a thing.

The worker then used the remainder of the session to discuss typical reactions to violent death, and presented guidelines which the parents could use to help their children cope over the coming weeks. She suggested that a healing step for both parents and child would be joint work on a memorial project.

Utilizing Raphael's (1983) and Bowlby's (1980) theory regarding variables influencing successful resolution of loss and bereavement, the workers were able to screen and identify those children who might be at risk for unusual or prolonged grief reactions. After the school vacation, the worker and the teacher met with the school administration to share the children's reactions to the death of their classmate, and to develop a follow-up plan for assessing the more vulnerable children. During this meeting, the worker provided the school with referral resources, such as local community mental health centers. Although the administration was initially reluctant to allow any type of memorial project, they agreed to talk with the committee of children and parents to share ideas. This represents the potential power of the classroom group to change the school environment to meet their needs.

THE SINGLE SESSION APPROACH

The single session group was elected due to time and schedule constraints, since the group structure (composition, leadership, and setting) could not be replicated with any degree of continuity to ensure adequate group process. Therefore, the worker chose to use the time constraints to the fullest degree, planning the group's work around the natural phases of beginning, middle, and end. The literature suggests that time limitations can have a telescoping effect on a group's work, and that the knowledge of a limited duration may encourage the group to reach its goal more quickly, and in less time than a group without such time limits (Block, 1985; Hartford, 1971). Clearly, from the above presentation, this seems true in practice.

The leader of a single session group must be comfortable with groups and have a flexible repertoire of skills. The worker must be able to "tune in to the needs of the group, negotiate a contract, create a demand for work, identify obstacles to mutual aid, and terminate" (Shulman, 1984) within a one to two hour period. Using the classroom teacher as a coleader in a crisis intervention group builds on a preexisting leader-member relationship, and encourages faster development of trust and group cohesion. In addition, worker is able to multiply herself by teaching her skills to the internal leader who will remain permanently with the group.

CONCLUSION

The intent of this paper has been to discuss children's responses of bereavement and loss following the violent death of a classmate, and to demonstrate how social group work skills can be effectively utilized to create a natural helping network within the classroom to provide social support and mutual aid. The broad framework of the mainstream group encourages intervention at those levels which have been touched by the death of a child. The result is an interplay of factors which promote change and growth during a period of crisis.

REFERENCES

Anthony, S. (1940) *The Discovery of Death in Childhood and After*. Middlesex: Penguin Books.

Bowlby, J. (1980) *Loss: Sadness and Depression in Attachment and Loss*. Volume 3. London: Hogarth Press.

Block, L.R. (1985) On the Potentiality and Limits of Time: The Single-session Group and the Cancer Patient. *Social Work with Groups* 8:81-99.

Brooks, B., Silverman, G. and Hass, R. (1985) When a Teacher Dies: A School-based Intervention with Latency Children. *American Journal of Orthopsychiatry* 55:405-410.

Erikson, E. (1968) *Identity, Youth, and Crisis*. New York: W.W. Norton and Co.

Getzel, G. and Masters, R. (1984) Serving Families Who Survive Homicide Victims. *Social Casework* 65:138-144.

Hartford, M. (1971) *Groups in Social Work*. New York: Columbia University Press.

McIntire, A., Angle, C. and Struppler, L. The Concept of Death in Mid-western Children and Youth. *American Journal of Diseases in Children* 123:527-532.

Miller, J. (1971) Childrens' Reactions to the Death of a Parent: A Review of the Psychoanalytic Literature. *Journal of the American Psychoanalytic Association* 19:697-708.

Nagy, M. (1948) The Child's View of Death. *Journal of Genetic Psychology* 73:3-27.

Papell, C. and Rothman, B. (1980) Relating the Mainstream Model of Social Work with Groups to Group Psychotherapy and the Structured Group Approach. *Social Work with Groups* 3:5-23.

Prichard, E. and Collard, J., eds. (1984) *Social Work with the Dying Patient and His Family*. New York: Columbia University Press.

Raphael, B. (1983) *The Anatomy of Bereavement*. New York: Basic Books.

Schwartz, W. (1961) The Social Worker in the Group. *Social Welfare Forum*: 146-171.

Shulman, L. (1984) *The Skills of Helping Individuals and Groups*. Ithaca: Peacock Publishers.

FROM THE WORLD OF PRACTICE

These two brief practice descriptions give powerful testimony to the feelings, ideas and beliefs that animate group work practice between workers and members. In some way the process of the group speaks for itself.

Sounds of Practice I:
Group Work with Rape Survivors

Susan Xenarios

Rape is a violent life-threatening crime where the perpetrator's intimidation and the victim's fear of death become part of an integral dynamic in the act itself. It is *not* a crime of passion provocated by a certain behavior or affect. It is one of power, control, denigration and premeditation. It is a violation, not only of the body, but of the psyche, and soul. Because it is an act of power and control, the human targets of rape have tended to be those who were perceived as the powerless and vulnerable. Therefore, women and children have historically been the primary victims of this crime. They still are. However, any professional working in this field quickly learns that rape is not exclusive to women and children alone. In fact, adolescent and adult males are entering emergency rooms and rape crisis centers in increasing numbers, identifying themselves as victims of sodomy and sexual assault.

The Rape Intervention Program at St. Luke's-Roosevelt Hospital Center was founded 10 years ago at a time when the Women's Movement and criminal justice system were urging medical treatment protocols, evidence collection and counseling services to meet the specialized needs of victims of rape. With the vital support of the community, a volunteer advocacy program was organized under the auspice of the Hospital Administration. This volunteer component was designed to meet the complicated medical and psychological needs of the rape victim and her/his family in the ER on evening, night and weekend hours. During the weekday shifts, ER social work, nursing, and now our program staff members, advo-

---

Susan Xenarios, CSW, is Social Worker at St. Luke's-Roosevelt Hospital, 114th Street and Amsterdam Avenue, New York, NY 10025.

95

cate and provide medical assistance, crisis counseling and ongoing support services.

As the ER social worker at that time, I counseled the rape victims who received treatment in our Hospital setting during the crisis period of recovery. It soon became evident, that recovery took several stages and often victim/survivors would return to me requesting a variety of different services; i.e., therapy, court advocacy, etc.

Many of these clients expressed the need to communicate with other victims of this crime. This was usually a period of "pseudo-adjustment" for them, where most of these women were functioning on a superficial and practical level by resuming their life activities, yet were feeling isolated, intermittently depressed, and exhibiting Mild PTSD symptoms. Our social values and mythologies often foster a premature pressure for the rape victim to quickly "return to normal." This is generally reinforced by the family, friends, and colleagues, as well as the victim herself. Unfortunately, this pressure also fosters a denial of the nature and impact this crime can have on a person and her world. Because of the aforementioned pressures on the survivor, we decided to organize short-term, goal-oriented support groups for these women. Through a process of trial and error, a group protocol was developed for a 12-week closed-ended treatment model. Although we experimented with shorter and longer numbers of sessions, the 12-session model seemed to be the "magic number" in accomplishing our goals, which are as follows.

To provide a safe-supportive environment of mutual aid, so that they can:

a. understand their reactions to their victimization, and
b. explore the issues and feelings arising from the rape so that they can begin to return to pre-trauma functioning.

Eligibility for group participation was open to any woman 18 years or older who had been a victim of rape. A pre-group interview was required for assessment purposes: i.e., level of pre-trauma functioning, quality of support network, ego strengths, history of prior victimizations, level of commitment to her own intrapsychic healing and some understanding of working within a group system.

Because of the intensity of feelings which surround this type of victimization, we felt it best to discourage women who had been raped within a 4-month period before the initial group session. For these women, a treatment plan of individual counseling was recommended. We remained flexible in terms of the length of time in which the rape had occurred. We have seen women in group where the longest span from the time of the assault to the beginning of treatment was 4 years.

THE GROUP

The group experience presented here consisted of 5 women ranging in age from 19 to 35 years. One participant was married, one recently divorced, the rest were single. All women received some professional support services immediately following the rape, i.e., medical, legal and 2 or more sessions of counseling. One woman was engaged in individual therapy prior to the rape. Two women went into counseling post-rape and continued through the course of the group.

Three members were college graduates, one was in a post-graduate program. Three were presently employed. One was a magazine editor, three were performing artists. One woman was Black and four were Caucasian. Only one member was a native New Yorker.

All of these women were verbal, angry and frightened. The nature of each rape differed greatly.

- D was mugged and raped by a stranger several blocks from her home while walking home from work.
- J was the victim of a "con" and was taken into a hotel room for a job interview. She was then held captive and repeatedly raped. She was a virgin.
- A was raped by two men who entered her summer home while she was in the process of moving her possessions into a van. She was raped and sodomized at gun point and was beaten, tied and bound, and tortured.
- C was attacked by a stranger who approached her asking for the time of day. She was dragged into an alley and was orally penetrated.

—H woke up in her bed to an unknown male assailant lying on top of her with a knife to her throat. She was vaginally, orally and anally penetrated. She sustained serious physical injuries.

Although there was a range of symptomatology, each woman experienced various degrees of the same symptom. For instance, each of these women was sporadically experiencing flashbacks of the attack, despite the time frame from the date of the victimization.

D said that "I've never acted like this before. A deadline comes by my desk, the pressure is on and all of a sudden, I think *"Wait a minute!!* What's important here. I was almost *killed*!! My mind flashes back and I'm immobilized."

H responded with her own flashback, "I was cutting up a chicken and blanked out. That was it. I became the chicken. I dropped the knife."

Periodic episodes of feelings of acute fear and vulnerability still permeated their consciousness and threatened their sense of emotional control which manifested in different kinds of behavior. After one year J was still unable to take a shower or bath when she was home alone.

After he raped me, I was bleeding. He told me I was dirty and to go to the bathroom to clean up and wait there. I waited and waited, shaking. It felt like hours. I thought he went to get friends and then he'd kill me. I didn't know that he left the Hotel. I was free and didn't know it.

A said, "I won't walk past any group of men huddled in a circle. I cross the street or walk around the block. Any group of strange men is a potential threat to me now."

All group participants had made significant changes in their lifestyles and patterns of daily living after their rape. H moved out of the apartment she shared with her roommate. D changed her wardrobe and style of dress. J married shortly after her rape, but discontinued drama school and her dance lessons. She stopped wearing make-up and changed her hairstyle. A, C, and H terminated their relationships with their lovers.

All of these women had imposed more rigid restrictions on their social lives and modes of transportation, i.e., public transportation was only taken during rush hours and taxis became an added expense in their budgets.

APPROACH

As the group facilitator, I always take a more active role in the beginning, introduction sessions.

My goal is to make the atmosphere warm, nurturing and safe enough for them to trust each other. Snacks and drinks are made available in the meeting room. My introductory style is to begin with the nonthreatening and concrete logistics, i.e., program's philosophy and history with this kind of group, general structure, confidentiality issues etc. I clarify why they're here and recognize that although the group cannot take away the rape, the hope is that the sharing of each other's experience and the main issues and concerns impacting on their lives now, will hasten the healing process. The anxiety, fear and pain in talking about this kind of violence must be openly acknowledged and validated.

People began to talk. Everyone needed to support or supplement their comparative experiences. Tears did not flow yet, but sadness and grief hung in the room.

As the assaults were recounted, women who had been strangers less than one hour ago reached out to touch another's hand or shoulder in comfort.

I labeled the sharing of grief as a beginning in the group process and that we would, over time, be able to turn the power of the assault into an instrument of empowerment.

In summing up this first session, it was understood that all was not said. We had just made a beginning. I asked the group to think of issues they would want to focus on in future sessions and reassured them that anyone could call me if they were having a difficult time. I closed by commenting on everyone's courage in coming forth with sharing their rape experiences, and asked them to begin to think of themselves as survivors from this session on. (There has recently been a move in the professional community to change the term from rape victim to rape survivor. This was thought to be more psychologically helpful in reaffirming survival skills.)

In leaving the office at the end of their session, personal safety became an obvious concern. I organized our departure so that no one traveled alone. It became an automatic group pattern by the next session. (Street, personal safety tips and techniques became topics to explore and role play over the weeks.)

As the group evolved and became more cohesive, trust became less an issue. The "fine and dirty" details of the assaults were shared and personal "secrets" disclosed. H revealed that her husband was a survivor of incest. J had been sexually molested as a child by her babysitter and never told anyone before this group. D shamefully revealed that her parents were survivors of the Holocaust. This piece of information was important to the entire group process as a springboard to further discussion on how they all minimized their own terror.

REFLECTIONS

In thinking about this 12-week group, the themes that seemed to repeat were: vulnerability, fear, guilt, shame, trust, safety, self-esteem and judgement. We were able, through the sharing of life stories, to affirm self-worth, encourage self-growth and conclude with a more positive view toward future plans and personal development.

Because of the material uncovered over the months, the group bonding was intense. At the final session, D cried for the first time since her rape. H said, "I feel the biggest thing the group has given me is that I feel I can trust and love again!!"

Phone numbers were exchanged and plans were made for a group dinner.

For me, this group experience showed me once again that it is indeed possible for women to survive, heal and grow.

Sounds of Practice II:
Group Work with Battered Women

Jane Seskin

As a social worker with the Crime Victim Assessment Project/
Rape Intervention Program, I work with battered women in individual counseling. My goal, stated at each intake, is as follows "I have
no stake in either pulling you out of this relationship or keeping you
in it. My only concern is in helping you stay safe."

One of the consequences of being battered is being isolated. The
battered woman lives alone with her secret. "How could I tell my
family and friends," asked F, "that my husband beat me? I was
ashamed he did it and ashamed I took it. How could I explain the
bruises? I just stopped seeing people. My husband thought that was
fine. He always cursed my family and made fun of my friends so
this fit in with his plans."

"How did you feel?" I asked.

"Cut off," she answered. "Alone with my problems and with
my pain."

As I listened to more and more women discuss their shrinking
worlds, I realized that F was *not* alone, but simply did not know
there were other women, just like her, struggling to stay safe and to
make change.

It was the Project's hope that a support group for battered women
would provide the opportunity for: (1) recognition that the isolation
was over; (2) exploration of feelings; and (3) encouragement of
practical and personal decision-making.

And so, for the past 30 Wednesdays, I've sat with 4 other women
and encouraged them to talk about violence. Two of the women in

Jane Seskin, MSW, is Social Worker at St. Luke's-Roosevelt Hospital, 114th
Street and Amsterdam Avenue, New York, NY 10025.

the group that formed from my caseload, hold white-collar jobs; one works part-time as a clerk typist and one is on public assistance. The youngest is 28 years old, the oldest 39. Two have children. One was out of her relationship when she joined the group, one made the break during the first month, another after 3 months in the group and the last member is planning to leave some time this week.

One group member continues to see me for individual counseling. Another calls once a week for what she's termed a "feelings check." The other two women schedule appointments on an "as needed" basis.

All have histories of battering (from 2-1/2 to 16 years). Collectively, the group has been slapped, choked, kicked, punched, scratched, bitten and hit with objects. They've been pushed down the stairs, thrown against the wall, knocked off chairs, and dragged out of bed. They've had knives, icepicks, bats, belts, and guns shoved in their faces. They've endured cigarette burns on arms, lacerations on scalps, and knife wounds on breasts. They've suffered bruises, contusions, and broken limbs.

At one time or another they've lost blood, hair, their dignity and a sense of hope.

THE PROCESS

The first group session was dramatically revealing of abuse. We'd gotten caught up in a game of "Can you top this?" As the women began to share their histories, it turned into a competition of who had suffered the most.

During the following week I wondered what the effects of this ventilation would be. I worried that no one would return. All did. One woman told how scared she felt. Another commented that at last she wasn't different.

We talked a lot that second session about safety and trust and the feeling of "letting go" with people who understood. We began to come together as a group.

We are a raucous, rowdy bunch. As the anger gets discharged, there's a lot of yelling, people talking at once, unexpected laughter and tears.

We are together for one reason; to talk about violence. As we peel away the layers, the urge to deny what happened is overpowering. "I'm tired of talking about anger," complained M one evening. "I want to talk about something pleasant."

"This is rough," I acknowledge. "But this is not some ladies' sewing circle. So for an hour and a half, one time a week, you and everyone else is to talk about, focus on and wallow in—violence and anger and everything tied up with this subject. You're here for a reason. You're a battered woman. That's your history and if you forget that history, your future's in jeopardy."

"Right on!" yells F.

We've begun 24 of the sessions with a go-round catch-up. Each member tells one good thing they've said or done that week and one thing they've experienced as a problem.

For 4 sessions I decided to experiment with the opening and instead began the session by throwing out a line to respond to (i.e., What do you think about this statement: "The batterer is not a loving partner"?).

Did they miss the go-round? The members talked of feeling "unhinged." They liked the idea of responding to something specific with their own examples, like the above statement, yet missed the opening structure. The go-round, T felt, gave her a feeling of "how each was handling her week." The other women agreed. M added, "I've always felt so out-of-control in my relationship that I look forward to sharing in the go-round. Whatever else comes up in group for me, I know I'm in control during the first 20 minutes." And so, it was unanimous and the go-round stayed.

Approximately every sixth session I'll distribute a handout; a T/F test on battering myths, a newspaper article on domestic violence, or perhaps a column by Ann Landers related to battering. The group reads and responds. There is in this way, additional reinforcement that they are not the only battered women out there.

Aside from the go-round and the occasional handouts, the hour and a half is up for grabs. When B decided she needed an Order of Protection against her husband, we gave most of the time to her plans. Or when M had her first date, she took an extended turn in the spotlight.

Over time, we've talked about feeling humiliated, degraded, insulted, out-of-control and powerless.

We've also talked about what it's like to be women, messages carried by the media, what and who are role models, family history, sex, jealousy, possessiveness, friends, the myth of machismo, raising children, assertiveness vs. aggressiveness, living alone, dealing with loneliness, self-esteem, being selfish, saying "No," learning how to meet new people, beginning to date, and feeling powerful.

We've used role-play to work through difficult situations. As the incidents (i.e., getting punched while walking down the street; confronting a blaming mother-in-law; reporting to the police, etc.) get acted out, there is immediate recognition leading to further revelations. Catharsis begins to occur as members respond sympathetically to each other's remembered pain.

Role-play has also been used to deal with issues occurring in the present and/or future. T takes the part of a schoolteacher while F portrays herself, a parent, enrolling her child in a new school. How much does she want to reveal of her history? What can she say to sensitize the teacher to her daughter's fears, a direct result of the violence in the home? F, previously anxious, begins to relax as B and M offer suggestions and support.

We've dissected past and present fights in order to understand some of the ingredients. Was there a point at which it could have been stopped? Was there something that could have been done to diffuse the situation before a fist was thrown? Were there buzz words to signal impending trouble? Who confronted whom? What constitutes provocative behavior? How does one "walk away"?

The "unsent letter" technique was used as an opportunity to deal with the abuser from a safe distance. Each woman wrote a letter describing the physical and emotional impact of the abuse and how she felt when it was going on. The letters were then read out loud. Comments ranged from: "Oh God, how did you stand it?" to "I think that was one of the hardest things I've ever done." After B read her letter she crumpled it up in a ball, dropped it on the floor and stamped it flat. The group watched in silence and then, as if acting on some unheard signal, they started to applaud.

I've tried, over the months, to create a frame of education, consciousness-raising and assertiveness training.

Weaving in and out over the weeks is the question, "Why do men batter?" The women answered in the following ways: (1) they can't help themselves; (2) they're angry; (3) he was drinking; (4) he was on drugs; (5) this is the way he shows he loves me; (6) this is attention; (7) he lost his job; (8) he shows who's boss; (9) he has to let off steam; (10) he's under a lot of pressure; (11) this is what men do; (12) he saw his father beat his mother; (13) he was beaten as a child.

No shrinking violet, I am in there, at each turn, trying to reinforce reality and what is and what is not appropriate behavior. "Whoa!" I've interjected, raising my hand. "Let's look at what you just said. Is that an excuse? A rationalization? Does it justify the hitting? Because I've got news for you. There is *no* excuse or rationalization for hitting someone."

There are moments when the air is thick with tension, the insults fly and the threat of violence hangs on an angry line tossed at another group member. The abusive relationship appears to be recreated.

"Let's slow down," I caution. "What's really going on here? Is it," I might ask someone, "what she said to you or the way she said it? Does it remind you of how you responded to _____? Try to think of what buttons are being pushed? What are you hearing? How are you feeling?"

In this way we look at the process, how the anger escalates and how it may be transferred and/or projected onto others. Working with this population is such an intense experience, the content so brutal and assaultive, that if I couldn't interject some humor into the sessions, all of us would have drowned in the bruises.

I've always used humor in my work with clients. It's been a way of dealing with painful truths; a method to touch the horror, back away and return for deeper examination. It's also been a way to break the tension and reduce anxiety. (In a discussion of safe sex I demonstrated how to use a condom by rolling one onto a cucumber. The women howled.)

Over time, the group has been able to kid each other, themselves, and me. In talking of an upcoming holiday and session cancellation, T reassured: "We'll be fine. We'll keep busy. We're getting so healthy that I've been waiting for a call from Donahue!"

Ambivalence. Why do women go back into abusive relationships? "Because," B says, "maybe this time it will work." There's often a feeling of hope that he will change, come to his senses, and/or realize he's doing something wrong. The reality is that every woman in the group left and returned to the relationship more than one time in the past.

"I guess," T told us, "at the time I went back it seemed easier to be with him than without. We'd been together 15 years. With him, I knew what to expect. I thought I'd be smarter, knew all his moods, knew when to duck when he got that evil look. He promised things would be different. They weren't."

"The casket is yours," stated M.

"Sounds ominous," I replied.

"Well," she continued, "I went back because of the kids. I thought they should have two parents. I thought by leaving he'd come to his senses. He'd realize how much he was losing. He didn't touch me for a week. And then he beat me so bad I thought I was going to die."

F added, "I hated being alone. I didn't know how to do it. Because of the relationship I'd alienated all my friends and family. It just seemed so hard to stay out."

"So instead of trying to deal with the loneliness, and instead of building a new life, you went back?"

"You got it!" she laughed. "No *I* got it. The next time he hit me he put me in the hospital. And then they gave me your name. And I'm out!"

"Yes," I agreed. "You're out."

Along with the ambivalence of going or staying, there is the ambivalence of loving and hating. The loving needs to be acknowledged. I asked the women to bring in pictures of their significant others. They described first dates, courtship, attraction, good times. "I remember," said M, "how funny he was. We used to go to places, do things, and I liked that."

Just as the anger can be held onto and used to help someone leave the relationship, the good feelings can be reminders of a possible future without violence.

I don't remember who first decided on the Gold Star system. I do know that we all use the line: "You get a gold star," when someone talks of an accomplishment. Gold stars have been given for: talking to an abusive lover without losing your temper; making an "I" statement; opening a savings account; getting a haircut; losing a pound. This throw-away line has become synonymous with recognition; we, the group, recognize the person has taken care of herself.

For 5 weeks we've talked about fun. Fun. Elusive, unknown. Was it the "ha, ha" kind: the sharing of something that occurred which brought forth laughter? Could fun be considered something pleasurable? Could it be a good feeling? Did fun have to cost money? Did one need others around to have the experience? Fun. What was it? How did it happen? And why, the group wondered, weren't they getting any?

For 3 weeks running I'd given them the assignment to "have some fun." There were no takers and the response was sheepish smiles and excuses, i.e., "I was too busy" or "I forgot."

"What are we talking about?" I asked, "what do we mean by fun?"

B shared a story of going to a party with her abusive husband. Aha! I thought. This was going to be fun. Wrong. B's husband got drunk, loud and argumentative. B felt embarrassed. She noticed that people moved away from her. She felt they were talking about her husband's behavior. B had on a new dress for the occasion. She wanted to dance, talk to her friends and yes, have some fun. But reality intruded on her expectations. "When he got like that I'd crawl into myself. I think I'd be waiting for him to start a fight. Usually I'd convince him to leave with me and we'd go home. Or sometimes, near the end, I'd just walk out and go to my sister's. I thought," she concluded, "parties were supposed to be fun. Well they never have been, in my experience."

M jumped in and described some of the parties she'd attended. Parties that sounded alive and joyful and fun. "So you see," she told B, "it's possible to go to one and have a good time."

"Perhaps," I wondered out loud. "It's up to each person to decide what having a good time means . . . just for themselves." I paused. "I was just thinking that maybe it's more complicated. Maybe you guys think you don't deserve to have fun, to have a good time."

"More punishment," suggested F. "You get in a cycle. The more he yelled at me, the more he hit me for no reason, well, I figured I must have done something to deserve it."

"And you didn't deserve anything good?"

"If you're repeatedly treated like shit," said B, "there's no way you're able to accept or even expect anything good to happen. Fun for me at this moment is just being alive and having my own space."

And perhaps, that's really what group is all about. Being alive and safe and having one's own space in which to grow. The fun part may be just being free to be without the threat of violence.

At the end of the session before my vacation, we all hugged each other. M told me: "I think what I like about you . . . is that you're so, so positive."

As I walked to the bus I thought about that statement. I realized that along with the weekly cookies, fruit, soda, coffee and tea that I provide, I dish out hope for a better life. I offer, through the group process, options and alternatives. I acknowledge the fact that they deserve more and that the power over their lives is within their grasp.